BEEKEEPING IN THE MIDWEST

BEEKEEPING
IN THE MIDWEST

ELBERT R. JAYCOX

CIRCULAR 1125

University of Illinois at Urbana-Champaign
College of Agriculture ● Cooperative Extension Service

This publication includes information about insecticides, chemicals, drugs, and other materials whose usage is regulated by state and federal agencies. Every effort has been made to provide information that is current and correct as of the date of publication. However, the status of some materials is not clear, and that of others may change at any time. Anyone using regulated materials, or planning to do so, should read and follow the label directions. If there is any question about the use of such materials, contact the extension apiculturist or extension entomologist in your state, or the local extension adviser or county agent. Beekeeping periodicals often include announcements about changes in the accepted uses of regulated materials by beekeepers.

So that the information in this publication may be more easily understood, trade names of products or equipment have been used in place of complicated descriptions or chemical identification. No endorsement of named products is intended, nor is criticism implied of similar products that are not mentioned.

This circular was reprinted April 1985 with minor revisions by E.E. Killion, Extension Specialist in Apiculture. Elbert R. Jaycox was Professor of Apiculture, University of Illinois at Urbana-Champaign, from 1963 to 1981. Photographs by the author and Killion.

Manufactured in the United States of America

CONTENTS

BEEKEEPING has been an important part of agriculture in the Midwest since about 1840. Early settlers and farmers kept bees in primitive hives or cut down bee trees to get honey for home use and for sale. In fact a dispute over bees once triggered the brief "Honey War" involving troops from Missouri and Iowa. A Missouri farmer set off the dispute when he cut three bee trees in the border area claimed by Iowa.

Honey bees have been selected and managed by man for many centuries. Nevertheless, they are still wild insects capable of living on their own without any assistance or special equipment. Probably because of this "resistance" to becoming domesticated, honey bees respond to beekeeping management practices in much the same way wherever they are kept. For this reason, the techniques discussed in this book are of use whether you live in the Midwest, in another section of the United States, or even in another country. Management must always be adapted to fit local conditions and to take into account the somewhat variable behavior of different geographical strains, or races, of honey bees. Differences in climate and sources of nectar and pollen, even over short distances, will force you to adjust your beekeeping methods, especially their timing, to the area in which you live. Wherever possible, the timing recommended in this manual relates to natural events such as plant bloom and seasonal temperature changes, which can be used as guidelines in temperate areas. They are not useful, however, in tropical or semitropical climates. Beekeepers, beekeeping organizations, and departments of agriculture are good sources of information about local conditions affecting honey bee management.

Beekeeping is continually changing, reflecting changes in cropping practices and agricultural land use. Commercial honey production now requires more extensive operations than in earlier days because nectar sources are more widely scattered. Fruit and vegetable growers, pressed by increasing production costs, are becoming more aware that the quality and quantity of insect-pollinated crops can be improved by renting bees for pollination. Providing bees for pollination is hard work, but it reduces the commercial beekeeper's dependence upon honey as the main source of income. After a period of decline, interest in keeping bees in urban areas has been renewed. Bees kept in cities improve yields in home gardens and orchards. Such colonies are often good honey producers because of the diversity of flowering plants available to them.

Learning to handle and manage bees is fun. It can also be confusing because advice given by any two authorities on bees is rarely the same. Fortunately, bees will usually prosper if you make sure they always have enough hive space and enough food. By joining state and local beekeeping organizations, you can share your experiences with others and increase your pleasure from keeping bees. For young people who are interested in starting to keep bees, there are beekeeping projects in 4-H and Future Farmers of America clubs.

BEES: THE INDIVIDUAL AND THE COLONY

The first step in studying bees is to learn as much as possible about their biology. This information about their life and needs is required to manage and maintain the colonies properly. It is even more important when you must diagnose an ailing colony that may have lost its queen or become infected with disease.

Kinds of Adult Bees

The honey bee colony includes both male and female bees for only a portion of the year. The males, or drone bees, are normally present in spring and summer. Female bees, the queen and her workers, are present all year. Naturally, all three types of individuals are important to the colony and to the survival of the species.

The beginning beekeeper needs to learn to recognize these different bees as quickly as possible. They are shown together in Figure 1. Close observation, repeated at frequent intervals, will make it easy to distinguish the two sexes and the two female castes.* The workers are the smallest bees in the colony. Their abdomens are pointed at the end but may vary somewhat in length. The abdomens of workers with full honey stomachs are longer than those of workers carrying little food, but they are always shorter than the queen's abdomen. Before the young queen mates, her body is similar in appearance to a worker's, except that its overall size is noticeably larger. As she begins to lay, the queen's abdomen becomes greatly elongated, so much that her wings look short. They cover only about two-thirds of her abdomen. In contrast, the wings of both workers and drones nearly reach the tip of the abdomen when folded. Queens' and workers' large, compound eyes are separated by areas of hair in which their three, small, simple eyes, called ocelli, are located. Drones have large, stout bodies with blunt abdomens. A conspicuous brush of hairs is visible at the end of their abdomens. This character is not present on the female castes. The drones' large, compound eyes can be easily distinguished from those of the other bees because they are the largest and they meet on top of the head. The drones' ocelli are located below the compound eyes, close to the antennae.

---

* All specialized terms are defined in the Glossary.

The three kinds of adult honey bees. The worker bee is at the top left, the drone is below the worker, and a marked queen is the large bee at the right. (Fig. 1)

The Workers

The worker bees (Fig. 2) are the largest group of bees in the hive — up to 60,000 in midsummer. They develop in the smallest cells in the comb of the colony from fertilized eggs laid by a queen. They are imperfect females and under normal hive conditions they do not lay eggs. The young, grublike or wormlike larvae receive large quantities of food that surround and support them for the first few days after they hatch from the egg. As the larvae grow, they consume all the excess food. The nurse bees then feed them small quantities of food at frequent intervals. About 5 days after hatching, the larva is sealed in its cell where it spins a partial cocoon and begins the body changes, or metamorphosis, that produce the pupa and finally the adult worker bee. The cell capping on worker cells is flat or only slightly convex. There are about 55 worker cells to the square inch, including both sides of the comb.

From 19 to 22 days after the egg was laid, depending on conditions in the hive, an adult bee emerges from the comb by chewing a hole in the capping of her cell. She is soft and downy, and is not yet capable of

A worker bee. **(Fig. 2)**

making wax, stinging, or flying. She will spend more than half her life doing hive duties in a rather flexible sequence that is governed by the colony's needs. Usually this begins with cleaning cells and feeding and caring for the brood (the immature stages of bees) (Fig. 3). Other typical duties include building comb, removing debris, and guarding the entrance (Fig. 4). Although we think of bees as being very industrious, the workers spend many hours patrolling the hive and sitting idle on combs. The patrolling probably serves to inform bees of the needs of the colony and also produces heat to maintain the warmth of the brood nest where the young bees are reared.

Young workers begin to fly from the hive when they are 10 to 20 days old, and in some cases even earlier. At first they take short flights in front of the colony, often on warm afternoons. These flights acquaint the bee with the appearance of the hive and its immediate vicinity. The term "play flights" has been given to this activity because the bees bob and weave in the air while facing the hive.

Workers forage first for either pollen or nectar. They may change from one to the other but usually collect pollen first and nectar later. The nectar collectors may also collect water when the colony needs it, and a few bees collect plant resins called propolis or bee glue.

Workers live 4 to 6 weeks during the active season. Those reared in the fall may live as long as 6 months, allowing a new generation to develop in the spring before they die. These differences in length of life have not been completely explained, but they are probably brought about by changes in glandular activity, diet, and the amount of brood reared by the colony in the fall.

A young worker bee feeding a larva. (Fig. 3)

Worker bees on guard at the hive entrance. (Fig. 4)

The colony uses large quantities of honey and pollen as food, but the bees usually store more honey than the colony needs. Only this surplus production should be removed by the beekeeper (see page 79). The young worker bee needs pollen to develop the glands that are used to make the secretions fed to developing larvae and to the queen. Adult bees can survive without pollen, but they are soon unable to rear young bees. Wax is produced by glands on the underside of the abdomen of house bees. It is secreted only when the colony is obtaining considerable quantities of nectar or is being fed sugar or honey by the beekeeper.

The Drones

The male bees, or drones, appear in the colony in late spring (Fig. 5). No certain number is produced and colonies may have only a few hundred or as many as several thousand. They help to produce heat in the colony and may be of value by affecting the "morale" of the colony or in other ways that are still not known. However, since they consume food and take up space, their numbers should be kept at a minimum. Colonies allowed to build combs without foundation or to repair damaged combs will produce large numbers of drone cells as well as worker cells. You can reduce drone production by using full sheets of comb foundation and by culling combs with large areas of drone cells.

The drone. Note the blunt abdomen and the eyes that meet on the top of the head. (Fig. 5)

The drones are produced from unfertilized eggs usually laid by a queen but occasionally by workers whose ovaries have developed (laying workers). A normal queen lays drone eggs in cells that are larger than worker cells. When sealed, the cells have distinct, rounded cappings (Fig. 6). Both laying workers and queens unable to lay fertilized eggs produce drones in worker-sized cells. Those that complete their development are normal, small drones, but many of them do not survive to maturity in the smaller cells. Drones require from 24 to 25 days to develop from egg to adult.

Another type of drone is produced in some honey bee colonies. However, they are never seen as adults because the worker bees remove them from the comb a day or two after the larvae hatch. These drone larvae hatch from fertilized eggs that have a matching pair of hereditary factors called sex alleles. The eggs are laid in worker-sized cells by a queen that mated with one or more drones having a sex allele the same as one of hers. Eggs with a single allele are unfertilized and usually laid by the queen in large cells of the comb where they produce normal drones. Fertilized eggs with two different sex alleles produce normal worker bees.

The production and loss of these drones, called diploid drones, is detrimental to a colony because as many as half of the fertilized eggs do not produce worker bees. The colony fails to develop the large population needed for honey production. A spotty brood pattern when no disease is present may indicate this problem, and the colony should be requeened.

Young drones are fed by workers for the first few days of their lives. After that time they help themselves to the stored honey and fly in search of queens on warm afternoons. Drones are attracted to certain small areas, at a considerable distance from their hives, where they congregate and patrol while flying 30 to 50 feet above the ground. It is here that they usually meet and mate with queen bees.

When flowers cease to provide nectar for the colony, either in the fall or, more rarely, at any time of the year, the workers no longer tolerate the drones. Workers remove developing drones from the comb and begin to harass the adults, the oldest ones first. The drones are rarely stung but they are pushed and pulled so much that they have difficulty eating. Ultimately, all the drones in a queenright colony are driven from the hive and die. The Italian race tolerates them longer than the Caucasians, and queenless colonies allow them to stay for an indefinite period.

Worker bees on sealed brood. The worker cells are at the top left and the drone cells at the bottom right. (Fig. 6)

The Queen

The queen (Fig. 7) is responsible for all the qualities of her colony. She mates with several drones and stores their spermatozoa within her body. These drones die, leaving the queen as their representative within the colony. The workers share the queen's motherly duties by caring for the young, but her genetic, or hereditary, makeup and that of the drones she has mated with determine the size and temper of the colony, the color of the workers and drones, disease resistance, honey-producing ability, and all the other characteristics of the colony.

Queens develop from fertilized eggs or from young female (worker) larvae not over 3 days old. In a colony that wants to swarm or needs to replace a failing queen, the old queen lays several eggs destined to become new queens in special cells, or cell cups, that hang vertically on the comb (Fig. 8). Worker and drone cells lie on a horizontal plane. When an old queen is lost, killed, or removed from a colony, the bees can produce a new queen from any worker larva not over 3 days old. To do this they modify the worker cell containing such a larva so that the queen develops in a vertical cell similar to those built from queen cell cups. Several queens usually are started at the same time. Regardless of the method by which she begins her development, the young queen larva develops much like a worker but does so more completely and more quickly, in only 15 to 17 days. She receives glandular secretions, called royal jelly, in excess quantity throughout her life. Queen larvae float in a bed of food. This greater quantity of food, together with other differences in quality and content, brings about the differences between worker and queen bees, and produces a queen that is a perfect female with a complete reproductive system.

When she emerges from her cell, the young queen is practically ignored by the workers. Very quickly, however, they are attracted to her and begin to feed and groom her. They even bite and chase her within the hive during the first few days. After about a week the queen is agile and physically ready for her mating flight. She leaves by herself, usually between noon and 4 p.m., and probably flies a considerable distance from the hive. It seems likely that queens visit drone-congregation areas because they mate with many drones in a short period. The average queen makes more than one mating flight and mates with as many as 10 different drones. This system of mating reduces inbreeding and thereby increases the efficiency of the colony.

The mated queen begins to lay a few days after completion of her flights. Her egg production increases rapidly to as many as 2,000 eggs per day. This high output, equal to the queen's own weight, is made possible by the high-protein diet of glandular secretions provided in large quantity by the worker attendants.

Queens lay eggs in greatest numbers in the spring and early summer. They gradually cease to lay in the fall and do not begin again until January or February. Winter brood rearing is normal and takes place in most colonies that have adequate stores of honey and pollen and a good population of worker bees.

Queens may live as long as 5 years but are most productive during the first 2 years. A common cause of failure is inadequate mating that results in the production of too many drones when the queen is unable to fertilize the eggs she lays in worker cells. At that time the colony usually tries to replace her by a process called supersedure. An old, failing queen and her young daughter may continue to live and lay eggs in the same colony for a considerable period.

Honey bee queen, marked on the thorax. (Fig. 7)

Queen cell cup being prepared by worker bees. (Fig. 8)

Length of Development

The three kinds of honey bees undergo the same type of development, known as complete metamorphosis. Each one takes a different length of time to develop as follows:

	Queen	Worker	Drone
		Day	
Egg is laid	0	0	0
Egg hatches	3	3	3-5
Cell is capped	7-9	7-9	9-10
Adult emerges	15-17	19-22	24-25

The Races of Bees

Throughout the world there are many races of bees that have developed slightly different body characteristics, biology, and behavior. In the United States two races of bees are most common — the Italian and the Caucasian. The Italian bees have yellow or brown bodies with varying numbers of dark bands toward the end of their abdomens. They tend to raise young bees early and late in the year and need more honey for maintenance than do the dark races. The Caucasian bees are black with gray bands of hair. They conserve their honey somewhat better and use more propolis than the Italian bees. Both races are usually gentle and the bees are quiet on the combs. Carniolan bees are a dark race with characteristics somewhat similar to the Caucasians.

The honey bees available in the United States are the result of crossing and selection of bees from many different races in addition to those mentioned above. Beekeepers should try queens from different queen breeders to learn more about the behavior and honey production of different strains of the same race. Most strains are gentle when handled under the proper conditions. If you have bees that are not gentle, requeen them immediately with a queen from a gentler strain. There is no relation between temper and honey production.

The Colony

Social insect colonies, including honey bees, have often been regarded as a single superorganism because groups of individuals appear to serve the functions of organs, and the colonies undergo changes as a group that compare with the lifetime development of an individual. To understand and manage honey bees you must be familiar with the development and activities of the colony, and the seasonal changes that take place in it.

The brood nest, where the queen lays eggs and young bees are reared, is the heart of the colony. It may be only a small circle of cells on one side of a comb, or it may include up to 20 or more full combs (frames). The areas occupied by brood on individual frames are usually oval or circular. The entire brood nest, including all the areas of comb containing brood, is generally ellipsoidal or spherical so that it is readily surrounded by the cluster of adult bees in cool weather. The bees form such a cluster when the temperature drops to about 57°F. (14°C.). The area containing developing bees, but not the rest of the hive, is kept at a temperature of about 95°F. (35°C.). The worker bees warm the brood nest to this temperature by moving their bodies and fanning their wings, activities that require honey as "fuel." In hot weather the bees cool the nest to 95°F. (35°C.) by fanning to evaporate dilute nectar or water present in the brood nest.

The bees store pollen, their protein food, in the cells immediately surrounding the brood (Fig. 9). In this location it is near at hand to be fed to developing larvae and to be eaten by newly emerged adult bees. The nectar and honey are stored beyond this band, or shell, of pollen.

In the fall, the brood nest and the majority of the bees are in the lower combs of the hive. The honey for winter food is above them and

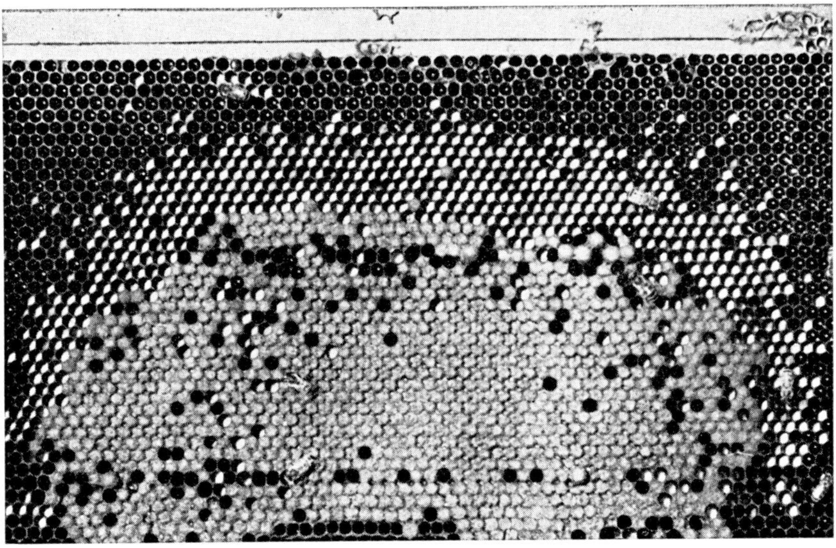

A comb with sealed brood in the center surrounded by a ring of light-colored pollen. Outer cells of the comb contain honey in open cells. (Fig. 9)

there must be pollen stored within the cluster area for winter use. This pollen and the developed food glands of the workers serve as a protein reserve for the colony until fresh pollen is available from spring-blooming plants. During the winter the bees in a hive of adequate size (at least two deep hive bodies) move upward as they gradually eat the stored honey. In early spring the brood nest is most often in the top part of the hive with empty combs beneath it. If nothing is done to change this arrangement, the bees will slowly occupy the lower combs, and the queen will expand her laying to all areas of the hive. However, the direction of natural expansion is upward, so the beekeeper usually rearranges the hive as explained on page 67.

Theoretically, one set of 10 deep combs is sufficient space for a prolific queen. In practice, 18 or 20 combs in two 10-frame hive bodies provide more suitable conditions for a large brood nest, perhaps because it can be more nearly spherical, rather than flattened as in a single hive body. The colonies need additional room for their rapidly increasing number of adult bees by late April or early May in central Illinois, or about the time of fruit tree and dandelion bloom. The nectar and pollen gathered from such plants may contribute to the crowding. The bees continue to store pollen near the brood nest and honey in the combs above it throughout the season. Without sufficient comb space, the workers gradually fill the cells of the brood nest with honey. This is highly desirable in the late summer to provide food for winter, but it is harmful earlier in the season when the greatest possible number of cells is needed for rearing young bees. The crowded brood nest restricts the queen's laying.

Worker honey bees have abilities that allow them to accomplish tasks that many other insects cannot do. They recognize several different regions of the color spectrum including near ultraviolet, which man cannot see. However, they cannot distinguish red from shades of gray and black. Honey bees detect polarized light and use it for orientation when foraging. Their senses of smell and taste are highly developed for most materials that are biologically important to them. They readily detect differences in concentrations of sugar solutions and distinguish minute differences in the components of mixtures of odors or solutions. Field bees learn the location of their hive and the appearance of landmarks around it. They also learn the daily movement of the sun in the sky and compensate for it when using the sun for orientation. Worker bees have a time sense, with a 24-hour base, that allows them to visit flowers or artificial food sources at the times when nectar and pollen are being offered. They can learn to associate a food reward with a flower scent after only one trial. Learning to associate color, time, and form (shape) with food takes 3 to 40 trials.

The honey bee colony has a simple system of communication that contributes to its success and adaptability. The system is based on the exchange of food among members of the colony (Fig. 10) and on odors released in and outside of the hive. The queen's glands secrete attractive substances and odors that are removed from her body and shared by the workers of the colony. The materials keep the colony together and prevent the workers from laying eggs and building queen cells. However, if there is an insufficient supply, or if it is not distributed evenly in a crowded colony, the bees construct queen cells to produce a new queen. Odors secreted by workers are used to attract other bees and to alert and alarm the colony. The fruity odor of the scent gland causes bees to cluster when swarming. It is also used when workers rediscover other bees, a queen, or the hive entrance after a period of confusion. Disturbed and injured bees secrete a volatile material known as isopentyl acetate that smells like banana oil. It attracts and excites bees and prepares them to defend the colony by stinging the cause of the disturbance.

A more complex means of communication may be present in the elaborate system of movements performed on the combs by bees when

Worker bees exchanging food on a comb containing honey. The two bees in the center are responding to smoke by eating honey from open cells. (Fig. 10)

they return to the colony after collecting nectar and pollen. These movements, usually called dances or the "language" of the bee, contain information about the distance and direction of the food source from the hive. They may also contain information about the quality, or sugar concentration, of the nectar. Although the idea of a bee language has been widely accepted, many scientists and nonscientists still do not agree that the language theory satisfactorily explains how bees recruit others to a food source. There is agreement that the movements contain information because it has been thoroughly decoded. But if there is truly a sophisticated language, it should bring recruits quickly and accurately to new food sources under a variety of conditions. Instead, the percentage of success is often low, the time in flight is far longer than needed for direct flight, and many bees fly the opposite direction from the food.

An alternative explanation proposes that odors of the food and of the aerial flight paths of foraging bees flying to it are used by newly recruited bees in finding food sources for the first time. This idea is supported by observations that few bees can be recruited to an odorless food source although foragers already visiting the food perform more frequent and vigorous dances in the hive than they do when collecting scented foods. More new bees, rather than fewer, should reach the food if the dances are the primary means of directing prospective foragers to a food source.

Two other observations bring the language theory into question. One is the effect of light wind, which does not interfere with flight, on foraging success of recruits. They do not find downwind food sources as well as ones upwind, indicating that odors borne by the wind outweigh the importance of information they receive from dancing foragers. Even a change in the number of bees visiting a food source from one colony can affect the success of recruits from another colony in finding the same source. When fewer bees from one colony fly to the food, fewer new recruits from a second colony are able to find it. Bees using a language should not be affected in this way. However, if the recruits are using the flight path to the food, such a path would have a weaker odor trail when fewer bees were flying along it.

It is natural, but not necessary, to relate the foraging success of honey bees to their use of a sophisticated language. Some stingless bee species use food odors and aerial odor trails and are even better able to exploit food sources rapidly than are honey bees.

One question commonly asked about the dance language is, "Why does the information exist if it is not used?" Similar information is present in the movements made by solitary moths after a flight. These movements continue for a period of time proportional to the distance the moth flew, yet there is no other individual that makes use of the information.

These controversial ideas are presented here to demonstrate that we do not know for certain all the facts about the activities of honey bees. More research is needed on the subject.

A communication system similar to the one bees use to find food is used to select a new home for a swarming colony. However, the relative importance of odor, flight paths, and "language" has not been fully clarified. Scout bees visit available cavities, such as a hollow tree, cave, or hole in a building, and evaluate their suitability as a home for the swarm. After many visits, the bees agree which one is best and move to it as a group.

Honeymaking

Bees make honey from several different sweet fluids that they collect from plants. Nectar, secreted by the nectaries, or glands, of flowers is the most common raw material, but some of it also comes from glands located on the leaves and buds of plants. This is called extrafloral nectar, and the glands are known as extrafloral nectaries. Honeydew is another sweet fluid that bees use to produce honey. It is surplus plant sap excreted by plant-sucking insects such as aphids and scale insects. Honeydew honey, called forest honey in Europe, is a wholesome product except when it is contaminated with mold or fungus organisms that darken it and lower its quality.

Nectar-collecting bees make trips ranging in duration from a few minutes to 3 or 4 hours. An average trip probably takes about an hour, and a bee may make as many as 10 trips per day. In order to get a full load of nectar, a bee may visit only one flower, such as that of saguaro cactus, or several hundred flowers, such as those of white clover. The nectar is carried back to the colony in the honey stomach, or honey sack. This is a storage organ in which no digestion takes place. It is controlled by the bee so that she can either regurgitate its contents or allow them to pass into her digestive system. She adds enzymes and waterlike secretions to the nectar from glands in her head. Nectar also contains plant enzymes, and honeydew includes enzymes of insect origin.

When the bee returns to the colony, she passes her load of nectar to one or more young house bees and returns to the field. The house bees do the primary job of processing the nectar into honey. This consists of repeatedly regurgitating droplets of the fluid onto the partly folded tongue held beneath the head. The bee continues this activity for 15 to 20 minutes, adding more glandular secretions and reducing the water content of the nectar. The resulting, partially ripened honey is placed in cells in the comb where it loses more moisture to the air circulated through the hive by fanning bees. When nectar is coming into the hive in large quantities, it cannot be processed immediately, but is stored as hanging droplets or as partly filled cells over a wide area of the combs. These small quantities of fluid lose moisture rapidly and are then processed and consolidated into full cells of honey. The filled cells are sealed with a capping of new wax.

Processing changes the raw material containing 25 to 40 percent solids, mostly sugars, into honey containing an average of about 83 percent solids. This rise in the percentage of soluble solids is proportional to the drop in moisture content. In addition to these changes in physical properties, extensive changes in chemical composition take place during processing. Nectar usually contains a mixture of two or three sugars: sucrose (common table sugar), dextrose (glucose), and levulose (fructose). During nectar processing, enzymes present in the fluid split most of the sucrose into the two simpler sugars, dextrose and levulose. At the same time, enzymes are also responsible for synthesizing other, more complex sugars and transforming some of the dextrose into gluconic acid, the primary acid in honey.

The final composition of different honeys is variable and complex, and differs according to the plant source. Sugars make up 95 percent or more of the solids present. The simple sugars (levulose and dextrose) account for nearly 70 percent, and levulose is usually predominant. As many as 12 complex sugars including maltose are present in small quantities. Although sucrose is often found in high concentration in nectar, as in nectar from the clovers, it makes up only 1 to 2 percent of honey on the average. Enzymes present in honey include invertase, diastase, catalase, and glucose oxidase. There are many acids in honey besides gluconic acid, and together they contribute to its noticeably acid reaction (pH about 4). Hydrogen peroxide in honey is a factor in the antibiotic properties of honey. This material and the high density and acidity of honey make it toxic to many disease organisms. Because most honeys are supersaturated solutions of dextrose, they are unstable as a liquid. The excess dextrose eventually crystallizes out of the solution in the process called granulation. Some honeys never granulate, while others granulate in the comb before they can be extracted.

Honey bees produce only comb honey, and the final product is sealed beneath a solid layer of wax cappings. However, man has never been satisfied to have only the single product, so there are different forms of honey whose names relate to the different methods of production and preparation for market. These forms include section comb honey, bulk comb honey, cut comb honey, chunk honey, liquid honey, and granulated honey.

Section comb honey is produced in small, square or rectangular wooden frames called sections. Each one holds about a pound of comb honey. Bulk comb honey is produced in shallow extracting frames, which can be sold as a unit containing several pounds of honey. Such comb can be cut into pieces called cut comb honey and sold in bags or plastic boxes. If the pieces are packed into jars and surrounded by liquid honey, they are called chunk honey. Liquid honey, also called extracted or strained honey, is separated from the comb by any of several methods. When honey solidifies it is known as granulated, crystallized, creamed, or candied honey. The granulation may be natural or the result of a special process described on page 90.

BEEKEEPING EQUIPMENT

Honey bees have been kept by man in a wide variety of hives. In the early days of the United States the most common hive was a section cut from a hollow tree, called a gum or log gum, with a slab of wood to cover the top of it. In Europe the straw skep hive was common and one model used in Greece had movable combs. In most other early hives it was not possible to remove or exchange combs easily because the bees glued everything firmly together and their combs were not surrounded by wooden frames. In 1851, L. L. Langstroth designed an improved hive that utilized a principle discovered earlier and now called the bee space. He made a hive in which the frames hung within a box so that they were surrounded on all sides by a space of ¼ to ⅜ inch. Bees leave such a space open but smaller spaces are usually filled with propolis. In larger spaces bees build extra comb. Langstroth's design is now used in all modern beekeeping equipment and, although the dimensions and some details have been changed, the hive is still called the Langstroth hive.

Bee hives have often been designed and built without regard for the needs and habits of the honey bee colony. Probably the best design for a colony was the large hive developed by Charles Dadant. It provided a large, deep brood chamber with plenty of room in which the queen could lay, and shallower supers for honey storage. However, the price and promotion of smaller hives offered for sale during the period from about 1885 to 1900 made them more popular. These small hives have since been blamed for the reduction in the numbers of farm apiaries because farmers removed too much honey from them, allowing colonies to starve during the winter. The 10-frame Langstroth-style hive has gradually become the standard hive used in the United States. It is essentially a compromise between the needs of the bees and a size one person can handle and move. As commercial beekeeping becomes more mechanized, there is less reason to limit the hive size and shape just for convenience in lifting and moving hives. But the amateur beekeepers will continue to need a hive whose parts they can lift, and the 10-frame Langstroth with shallow supers fills this need.

Many beekeeping enthusiasts are attracted by unnecessarily elaborate equipment or feel a need to modify the basic Langstroth design.

Most items designed for this purpose are of little value. Knowledge of bees and the ability to manage them are the two essentials of success with bees. It is the strong colony of bees, properly managed, that makes the honey, not some special piece of hive equipment. Use standard items of equipment to enjoy beekeeping to the fullest extent. If you should want to sell or exchange the equipment, you can do so more easily with conventional hives.

Hive Parts and Selection of Equipment

A bee hive is composed of one or more wooden shells called hive bodies within which hang the combs in wooden frames. The space between the cover and the bottom board can be expanded or reduced to meet the needs of the colony during the year. Hive bodies in which a brood nest is located are usually called brood chambers. Hive bodies located above the brood chamber are called supers, simply because of their location above the brood nest. The hive may be made up of any combination of hive bodies of the same or different vertical dimensions, or depths. Traditionally, beekeepers have used brood chambers at least 9⅝ inches deep, but honey bee colonies will live just as well when given sufficient combs of shallower dimensions. Amateur and commercial beekeepers should seriously consider using hives composed entirely of 10-frame hive bodies 6⅝ inches deep (Fig. 11). They provide complete interchangeability, are lighter in weight, and are easier to manipulate. All the parts of a hive should be the same width, preferably 10-frame. The parts of a bee hive are shown in Figure 12.

Hive composed of two, Dadant-depth shallow hive bodies. (Fig. 11)

Parts of a typical bee hive. The parts have been separated and identified for easier recognition. (Fig. 12)

Bee hives are available from many different companies (see page 155) or you can make your own. If you prefer to build them, make sure that all dimensions of the hive bodies conform to those of commercially built hives. Otherwise the bees will fasten the parts together so firmly that you cannot manipulate them easily. Hive covers and bottom boards need not necessarily be of the same pattern as commercial ones. Simpler ones can easily be made at home, and plans for constructing them and other parts of a hive can be found on page 38.

Beekeeping suppliers and catalog stores offer basic equipment kits for beginners. The kits contain only the basic tools and equipment needed to get a swarm or package of bees started and to provide hive space for them for about a month in the spring. Purchase additional equipment at the same time in order to be ready to provide space for the colony to expand during the season. Without additional hive bodies the bees will soon become crowded and swarm. They may never develop a sufficient population and a supply of honey to survive the winter. In that case you will have to start over the next year. If you do it right the first time with adequate equipment, you may soon be wondering what to do with all the honey.

The type of equipment you should select depends, in part, on the type of honey you plan to produce. The beginner is wise to avoid producing section comb honey because it requires specialized management and an abundant nectar flow for good returns. Management for producing cut comb honey (Fig. 13) is simpler, the returns are generally better, and the equipment for producing it can also be used interchangeably for producing extracted honey. For these reasons, section comb honey production is not included in this book. Details concerning its production can be found in sources listed on pages 154 to 156.

No matter which type of honey you want to produce, plan to use at least two hive bodies 9⅝ inches deep or three hive bodies 6⅝ inches deep for the brood chamber. Above this brood chamber you will need two to four hive bodies, or supers, for honey storage. To produce cut comb honey, give the bees shallow supers, 5 11/16 inches or 6⅝ inches deep, with frames containing cut comb foundation without wire reinforcement. The term "comb foundation" refers to sheets of beeswax embossed with the worker cell pattern. Bees add wax to the foundation to make a complete comb. Extracted honey can be produced in supers of any depth. The frames should contain wired or plastic-base foundation. The 6⅝-inch-deep supers, sometimes called Dadant-, Illinois-, or medium-depth supers, are a good size. They are lighter in weight than deep, 9⅝-inch supers, but you do not need as many of them to hold

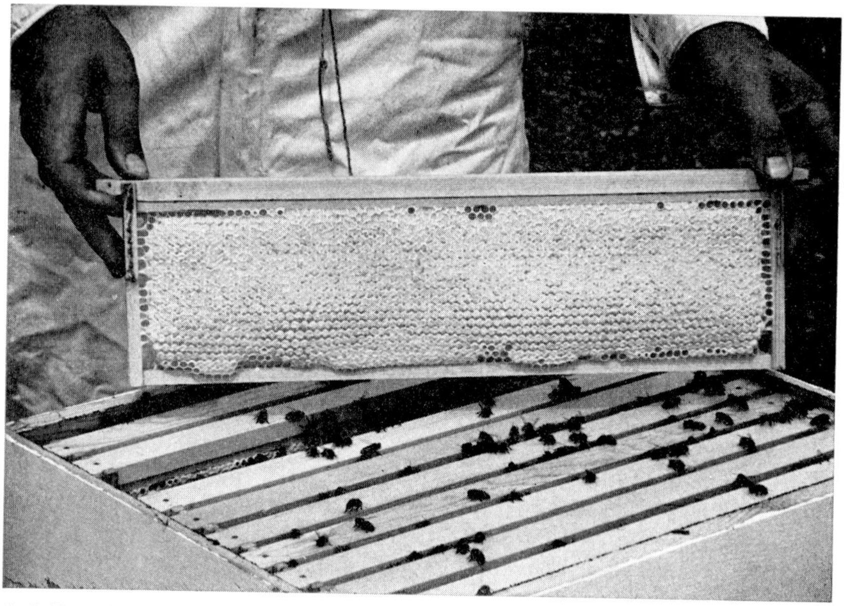

A full shallow comb of honey. The comb and frame may be sold as a unit or the comb may be cut into pieces for cut comb or chunk honey. (Fig. 13)

the crop as you do of the standard shallow, $5^{11}/_{16}$-inch supers. Many beekeepers in the western states use only deep supers. Although they must handle heavier units weighing up to 90 pounds, they handle fewer of them, and all the equipment is interchangeable.

Of the several styles of frames, those with a wedge top bar and a split or slotted bottom bar are the least trouble for the beginner to use with supers of any depth. Foundation slips quickly into this frame and it will stay secure when the wedge is nailed in place. Plastic-base foundation can be stapled in place or held with a wedge. If it is stapled, an extra row of cells for honey storage is gained on each frame.

There are two basic types of comb foundation, distinguished by their relative thicknesses. Brood foundation, often called medium brood, is used for the brood chamber and in all frames used to produce extracted honey. Its thickness, especially when reinforced with wire or plastic, helps make strong combs that can withstand many years of use. Plain and wired foundation make the best combs when placed in wired frames; plastic-base foundation does not require any wiring. Foundation for honey to be eaten in the comb must be thinner and more delicate than brood foundation. The thinnest one, for comb honey produced in sections, is often called thin super or thin surplus foundation. The easier and faster (Fig. 15). Drive nails down through each end of top bar into the end bars and drive a second pair through the end s into the shoulder of the top bar (Fig. 16). This cross-nailing tly strengthens the frame. Glue and power-driven staples can also ised to assemble frames. Water-resistant casein glue and polyvinyl ite) glue are easy to apply with a plastic squeeze bottle. The bottom needs two or four nails, depending on the style of frame. Frames one V-shaped edge on the end bars are assembled with the V ng you on the left end and away from you on the right end.

rames are wired (Fig. 17) to reinforce the combs so that they will sag and warp in hot weather or fall apart in the extractor. If you d to keep more than a half dozen colonies or if you like to learn techniques, you should learn to wire frames. A plan for a wiring l can be found on page 40. Using such a wiring device, thread at two, and preferably four, horizontal wires through the ready-made in the end bars. Draw the wire tight enough to make a high note you pluck it. Start and end the wire by wrapping it around small driven into the edge of the end bar. Only No. 28 tinned wire is le for wiring frames. If the wire cuts deeply into the end bars, metal eyelets into the holes or use a compression stapler to put a beside the holes.

ling frames in a wooden jig. The jig is inverted to put the bottom lace. (Fig. 15)

foundation for cut comb honey, sold by that name, is slightly thicker so that it will stay in place in the frame until made into comb. These thin foundations are used without wiring so that the filled honey comb can be cut from the frames ready to eat. Support pins or bobby pins can be inserted through the frame ends to help hold the foundation in place. The pins are pulled out of the frame at harvest time and can be reused.

When bees are provided with comb foundation, they must have incoming nectar or sugar syrup to secrete wax and build comb. Otherwise they may cut holes in the foundation and fail to make it into comb. For this reason you must feed any new colony started with sheets of foundation. Add foundation to established colonies only during a nectar flow or while they are being fed syrup. Always use full sheets of foundation, not just strips.

Hive covers are of two basic types. One telescopes down over the hive body and is used above a flat inner cover to keep the bees from attaching it too tightly to remove (Fig. 14, top). The other type of cover fits flush with the sides of the hive body, and may or may not extend over the ends. These simple covers are made in several styles. They may be constructed of a single piece of ¾-inch-thick exterior plywood or several pieces of wood joined together and covered with metal. Other patterns have one or two cleats at either end (Fig. 14, bottom). The telescoping cover is heavy and expensive. It creates problems when hives are moved because the hives do not fit closely together on a truck, and they will break open when roped tightly in place. However, the cover provides some insulation and ventilation for the colony and resists weathering well. Plain covers are less expensive and easier to make than telescope covers. They save time in manipulating colonies, stay in place well, weigh less, and are best suited for migratory beekeeping.

The hive bottom, or bottom board as it is called, is also made in two basic types. One is reversible, with a deep and a shallow side to give either a ⅜-inch or a ⅞-inch entrance to the hive (Fig. 14, top). It has long siderails that sit on the ground. The other type is constructed much like a simple cover, with cleats at front and back (Fig. 14, bottom). The brood chamber sits on strips of wood whose height governs the height of the entrance. A ⅜-inch entrance is most common, but deeper ones can easily be provided by varying the height of the wooden strips. This bottom is easier to make, lighter in weight, and usually less expensive than the reversible one. Hive bottoms should be nailed or stapled in place if the hives are moved. Otherwise the hive bodies are just stacked one above the other on the bottom board. Bottom boards

A one-story hive with a telescoping cover and a reversible bottom board is shown at the top. Another one-story hive with a plain cover and two-cleat bottom board is shown in the bottom illustration. (Fig. 14)

will last much longer when soaked or brushed wi
approved for such use before being painted.
any preservative material directly harmful to be
ingredients such as insecticides that will kill bees.

Hives placed on a hive stand, on bricks, or
at a little more convenient height for the beek
trances to the hives are also less liable to be cov
that can interfere with hive ventilation and
colony in hot weather. On the other hand, hiv
advantage. A queen that falls to the ground d
clipped queen that tries to leave with a swarm
back into the elevated hive. When several hiv
manipulation of one colony may disturb and
with preservative-treated bottoms are damag
the ground, and the preservatives do not bothe
beekeepers and others who move their hives re

The design of beekeeping equipment has
years, but equipment is now being made in f
materials. Hives, frames, excluders, and comb
Some of this equipment has warped in use,
have not been well accepted by the bees. I
tinually being improved, and its use will pr
the relative prices and availability of woo
should test the new materials and determ
whether they have advantages over the tradit

Assembly of Equipment

New bee equipment is usually purchase
or unassembled. The directions and diagra
facturer are easy to follow, but a few detail
A common error is to nail the sides of the
handholds on the inside. The frame rests
at the inside top of the hive ends) also caus
from some suppliers requires the additic
across the frame rest to give the proper ve
Other manufacturers supply a bent metal
stalled so that it projects upward from t
the inside of the hive body.

Frames are made in several sizes and
in the same way. You can assemble smal
ually. For larger numbers, a frame-nailir

job
the
bar
gre
be
(wh
bar
wit
faci

not
inte
new
boar
least
holes
when
nails
suita
inser
stapl

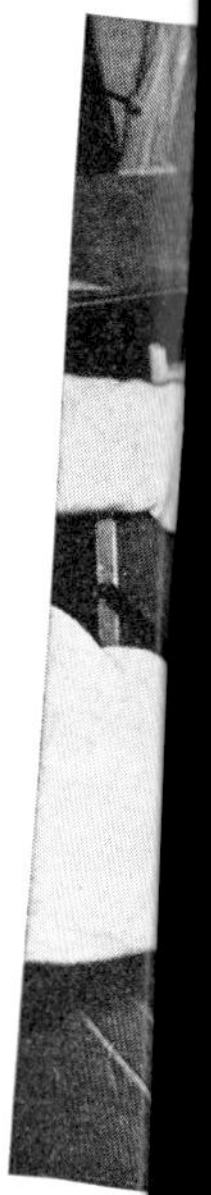

Assem
bars in

foundation for cut comb honey, sold by that name, is slightly thicker so that it will stay in place in the frame until made into comb. These thin foundations are used without wiring so that the filled honey comb can be cut from the frames ready to eat. Support pins or bobby pins can be inserted through the frame ends to help hold the foundation in place. The pins are pulled out of the frame at harvest time and can be reused.

When bees are provided with comb foundation, they must have incoming nectar or sugar syrup to secrete wax and build comb. Otherwise they may cut holes in the foundation and fail to make it into comb. For this reason you must feed any new colony started with sheets of foundation. Add foundation to established colonies only during a nectar flow or while they are being fed syrup. Always use full sheets of foundation, not just strips.

Hive covers are of two basic types. One telescopes down over the hive body and is used above a flat inner cover to keep the bees from attaching it too tightly to remove (Fig. 14, top). The other type of cover fits flush with the sides of the hive body, and may or may not extend over the ends. These simple covers are made in several styles. They may be constructed of a single piece of ¾-inch-thick exterior plywood or several pieces of wood joined together and covered with metal. Other patterns have one or two cleats at either end (Fig. 14, bottom). The telescoping cover is heavy and expensive. It creates problems when hives are moved because the hives do not fit closely together on a truck, and they will break open when roped tightly in place. However, the cover provides some insulation and ventilation for the colony and resists weathering well. Plain covers are less expensive and easier to make than telescope covers. They save time in manipulating colonies, stay in place well, weigh less, and are best suited for migratory beekeeping.

The hive bottom, or bottom board as it is called, is also made in two basic types. One is reversible, with a deep and a shallow side to give either a ⅜-inch or a ⅞-inch entrance to the hive (Fig. 14, top). It has long siderails that sit on the ground. The other type is constructed much like a simple cover, with cleats at front and back (Fig. 14, bottom). The brood chamber sits on strips of wood whose height governs the height of the entrance. A ⅜-inch entrance is most common, but deeper ones can easily be provided by varying the height of the wooden strips. This bottom is easier to make, lighter in weight, and usually less expensive than the reversible one. Hive bottoms should be nailed or stapled in place if the hives are moved. Otherwise the hive bodies are just stacked one above the other on the bottom board. Bottom boards

A one-story hive with a telescoping cover and a reversible bottom board is shown at the top. Another one-story hive with a plain cover and two-cleat bottom board is shown in the bottom illustration. (Fig. 14)

will last much longer when soaked or brushed with a wood preservative approved for such use before being painted. Be careful not to use any preservative material directly harmful to bees or one that contains ingredients such as insecticides that will kill bees.

Hives placed on a hive stand, on bricks, or on other supports are at a little more convenient height for the beekeeper to work. The entrances to the hives are also less liable to be covered by grass and weeds that can interfere with hive ventilation and cause the death of the colony in hot weather. On the other hand, hive supports can be a disadvantage. A queen that falls to the ground during manipulation or a clipped queen that tries to leave with a swarm may not be able to get back into the elevated hive. When several hives are on a single stand, manipulation of one colony may disturb and alert the others. Hives with preservative-treated bottoms are damaged little by being set on the ground, and the preservatives do not bother the colony. Commercial beekeepers and others who move their hives regularly do not use stands.

The design of beekeeping equipment has changed little over many years, but equipment is now being made in fewer styles and with new materials. Hives, frames, excluders, and combs are now made in plastic. Some of this equipment has warped in use, and other types of plastic have not been well accepted by the bees. But the equipment is continually being improved, and its use will probably be limited only by the relative prices and availability of wood and plastic. Beekeepers should test the new materials and determine in their own apiaries whether they have advantages over the traditional ones.

Assembly of Equipment

New bee equipment is usually purchased "knocked down" (KD), or unassembled. The directions and diagrams furnished by the manufacturer are easy to follow, but a few details sometimes cause difficulty. A common error is to nail the sides of the hive bodies in place with the handholds on the inside. The frame rests (notched or rabbeted areas at the inside top of the hive ends) also cause some problems. Equipment from some suppliers requires the addition of a small wooden strip across the frame rest to give the proper vertical spacing of the frames. Other manufacturers supply a bent metal frame rest that must be installed so that it projects upward from the rabbeted area, not toward the inside of the hive body.

Frames are made in several sizes and patterns, but all are assembled in the same way. You can assemble small numbers of frames individually. For larger numbers, a frame-nailing device or jig will make the job easier and faster (Fig. 15). Drive nails down through each end of the top bar into the end bars and drive a second pair through the end bars into the shoulder of the top bar (Fig. 16). This cross-nailing greatly strengthens the frame. Glue and power-driven staples can also be used to assemble frames. Water-resistant casein glue and polyvinyl (white) glue are easy to apply with a plastic squeeze bottle. The bottom bar needs two or four nails, depending on the style of frame. Frames with one V-shaped edge on the end bars are assembled with the V facing you on the left end and away from you on the right end.

Frames are wired (Fig. 17) to reinforce the combs so that they will not sag and warp in hot weather or fall apart in the extractor. If you intend to keep more than a half dozen colonies or if you like to learn new techniques, you should learn to wire frames. A plan for a wiring board can be found on page 40. Using such a wiring device, thread at least two, and preferably four, horizontal wires through the ready-made holes in the end bars. Draw the wire tight enough to make a high note when you pluck it. Start and end the wire by wrapping it around small nails driven into the edge of the end bar. Only No. 28 tinned wire is suitable for wiring frames. If the wire cuts deeply into the end bars, insert metal eyelets into the holes or use a compression stapler to put a staple beside the holes.

Assembling frames in a wooden jig. The jig is inverted to put the bottom bars in place. (Fig. 15)

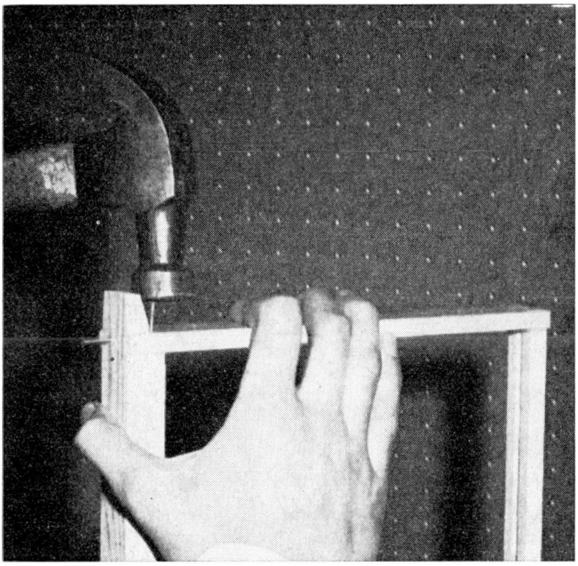

Cross-nailing the end and top bars of the frames.
(Fig. 16)

The alternative to wiring is the use of plastic-base or vertically wired foundation with metal support pins to hold and center the foundation at the end bars of the frame. Combs produced in this way should be handled and extracted carefully, especially in hot weather, until they are fully finished and have been in use for at least one season. Hold the combs vertically when you examine them so that the new comb will not sag or fall from the frame because of the weight of brood or honey.

Fit foundation into a frame so that the upper edge rests in the notch in the top bar and the lower edge rests in the slot of the bottom bar. The foundation in a wired frame should lie on top of the wires. Place wired foundation so that the bent ends of the wires will be held in place by the wedge. Push the wedge firmly into place against the foundation and nail or staple it so that the nail heads or staples are beneath the top bar (Fig. 18). Here they cannot later be hit with an uncapping knife. Plastic-base foundation can be held in place with staples or a wedge (Fig. 19).

When frames are wired, the wires must be embedded in the wax so that they are acceptable to the bees. Otherwise the bees may build irregular cells along the wires or fail in other ways to make a perfect comb. Place the wired frame and foundation, wires up, on a board cut to fit within the frame. Roll a heated spur embedder along each wire, pushing it about halfway through the wax or against the vertical wires (Fig. 17).

The foundation should be warm. For large numbers of frames, use an electrical embedder with a 12-volt transformer to heat the wires so that they sink into the wax (Fig. 20). Use it briefly and carefully to avoid cutting the foundation into strips with overheated wires or melting holes in the wax where wires cross. Plans for an electrical embedder and embedding board can be found on page 43.

Wiring frames in a homemade wiring device. A deep frame compressed with a metal clamp is shown in the illustration at the top. Bottom illustration shows the spur embedder. (Fig. 17)

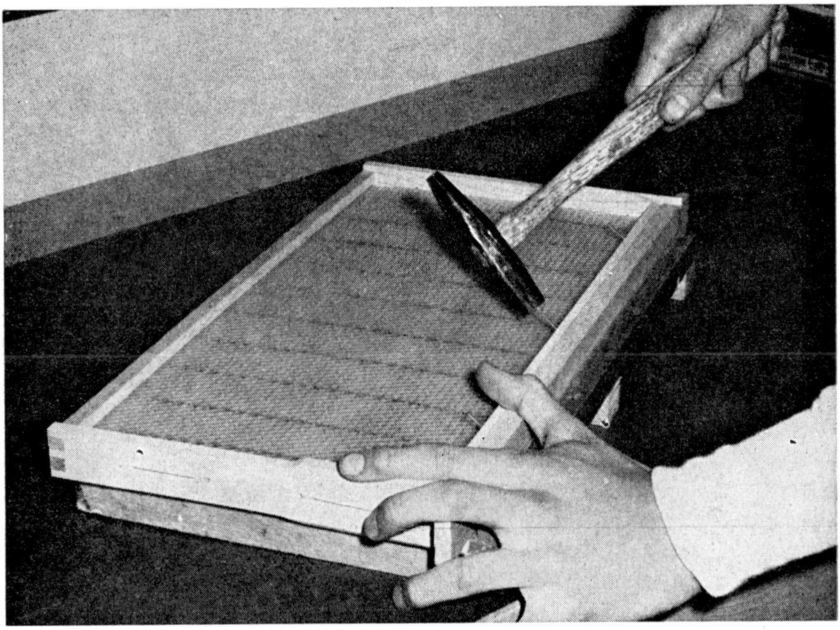

Nailing the foundation cleat in place in a frame. (Fig. 18)

Using a compression stapler to fasten plastic-base foundation in a shallow frame. (Fig. 19)

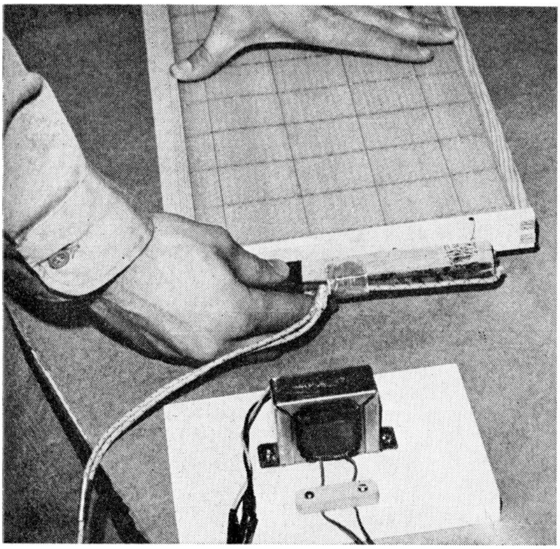

A simple device for embedding wires into comb foundation. When the copper contacts at each end of the wooden piece touch the wires on the frame end bar, the heated wires sink into the wax. (Fig. 20)

After assembly, the external wooden hive parts should be treated to increase their usable life. Bottoms, and other hive parts, can be soaked or coated with a suitable type of wood preservative that can be painted over. In some countries hive bodies are preserved by dipping them for 10 minutes in paraffin heated to the smoking point (316°F., 158°C.). Hives can be painted with either latex or oil-base paint. They should be painted inside and out. This reduces peeling and loss of paint caused by moisture in the wood and does not harm the colony in any way. White paint reflects heat better than darker colors or aluminum paint. The light color helps colonies stay cooler in hot summer weather. Foraging bees find their own hives more easily when they are distinguished by different colors painted near the entrances. The color combination of blue, yellow, white, and black is a good one for this purpose.

Tools, Specialized Equipment, and Clothing

Three essential beekeeping tools are shown in Figure 21. The smoker is your most important tool. With it you are master of the bees as long as you use it properly and keep it lit. The 4 × 7-inch size is the best of the three sizes available. Smaller ones are too small even for beginners and the largest size is designed for commercial beekeepers.

Hive tools are all-purpose levers for prying hives apart and for scraping. The 10-inch length gives the best leverage when hives are heavy and stuck tightly together.

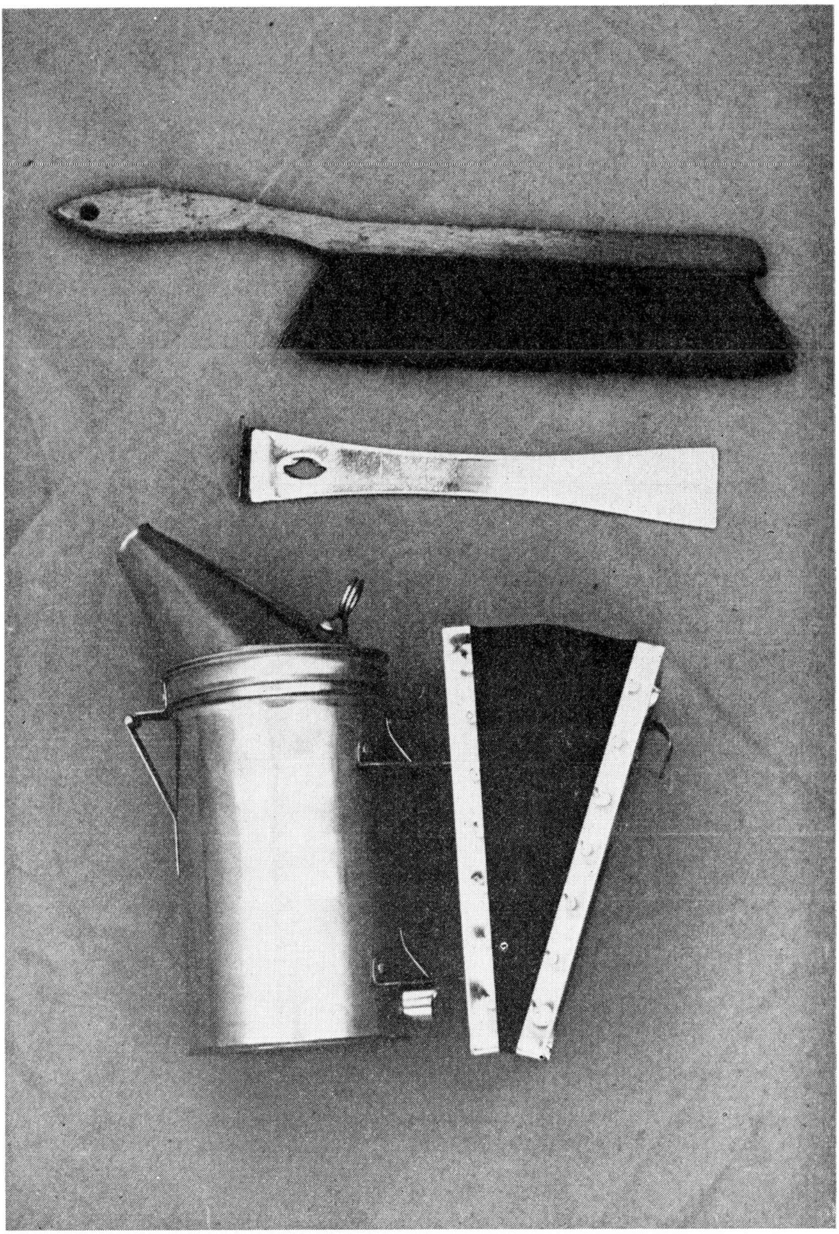

Three important tools in beekeeping. The bee brush is at the top, the hive tool in the middle, and the smoker at the bottom. (Fig. 21)

A bee brush is used to remove bees from combs of brood or honey, particularly those bees that don't come off when the comb is shaken. Since queen cells may be damaged by shaking, a brush is a necessity in queen rearing. If a brush isn't handy, a handful of long grass can be used as a substitute.

A queen excluder is a grid of accurately spaced holes or wires through which workers can pass, but not queens or drones. The steel-wire excluders, either metal or wood bound, are best. The zinc and plastic ones are suitable only for temporary use or for special purposes such as making cages or covering hive entrances.

Always use standard hives without modification or accessories. Special bottom boards and covers, queen and drone traps, and other similar equipment usually increase the cost of keeping bees without providing proportionate returns. It is proper management, not specialized equipment, that leads to success in beekeeping.

It is not necessary to wear extra layers of clothing when working with bees but it is a good practice to dress properly, at least until you gain experience. Bee gloves, either cloth or leather, help to put you at ease in handling frames of bees. Simple gauntlets let you use your fingers more easily than do gloves, yet cover your wrists and the opening in your sleeve above the cuff (Fig. 22). A muslin sleeve with elastic in each end makes a good gauntlet. Make it long enough to reach from your thumb to above the elbow. You can also cut the toe or foot from a large, white, cotton sock and pull it over your sleeve with the knitted top on your wrist.

White or tan clothing is most suitable when working with bees. Other colors are acceptable but bees react unfavorably to dark colors and fuzzy materials. Be especially careful to cover your ankles or wear light-colored socks. Angry bees often attack ankles first because they are at the level of the hive entrance. Any bee on the ground tends to crawl upward and may go up your leg with peaceful intentions until you squeeze her. Use bicycle clips, inner-tube bands (Fig. 23), or string to fasten your pants legs.

A folding wire veil or a round wire veil, worn with a hat, is a good all-purpose choice for the beginner. A nylon net veil is cool and easy to carry, but it is more easily damaged in use. Wear the veil on a hat with a wide brim and pull the excess material away from your neck when putting it on. Instructions for making a nylon net veil can be found on page 51.

A pair of gaunlets in use. They can be used alone or with a pair of gloves.
(Fig. 22)

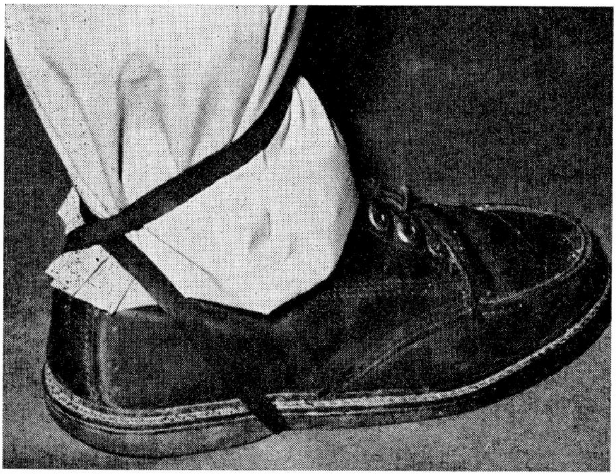

An inner-tube band for closing pant legs when working with bees. The band closes and pulls down the pant leg.
(Fig. 23)

Making new Illinois supers. (Fig. 24)

Making Your Own Equipment

There are several reasons why people make their own beekeeping equipment. They may want to reduce the cost of getting started in beekeeping or they may simply enjoy working with their hands (Fig. 24). In many cases they want a special item that is not readily available or, if it is, the product is not suited to their needs. The plans and instructions in this section will enable you to make some of your own equipment. Before doing so, you should compare the labor and material costs of making a piece of equipment with the delivered price of the same item from a bee supply company. The price of high-quality lumber used in commercial bee supplies may make it difficult for you to save money unless you produce a lower quality product from less expensive materials.

Constructing a bee hive. Bee hive construction is not difficult for a person with suitable woodworking tools and experience in operating them. The equipment produced can be as satisfactory as the commercial products, provided that all dimensions are accurate (see construction plan on page 38). The *inside* dimensions of the hive bodies and the size of the frames are especially important so that the completed hive provides the proper bee space — the space that bees keep free of comb and propolis. Without proper dimensions, the movable frames quickly become immovable and difficult to manipulate when filled with bees. The construction plan shows the inside dimensions for the deep hive body only. Those for the other hive bodies differ only in depth, which is the same inside and out. The external dimensions given are suitable only for equipment constructed from ¾-inch-thick lumber. Adjust the dimensions if you use wood of any other thickness.

Western pine is the best wood to use for hive bodies, lids, and frames. Many other woods can be used, but most are less suitable because of their weight, tendency to crack and split, and other characteristics. Hive bottoms made of cedar, cypress, or redwood generally last longer than those made of pine or similar woods. Regardless of the type of wood used, hive bottoms resist moisture and decay better if they are treated with a wood preservative.

Bee equipment may be assembled with nails or power-driven staples. Seven-penny box nails, cement or resin coated, are a good size for hive bodies. The corners of the hive bodies should be cross-nailed for greatest strength. Galvanized nails are a good choice for assembling bottoms and for use with redwood lumber. Coated box nails, 1¼ inches long, are suitable for nailing frames. Glue makes all wooden equipment stronger and longer lasting.

You may wish to consider some optional ways of making the different parts of a hive. For example, lids can be made of exterior plywood without cleats. Or the lid can be lengthened to accommodate a ¾ × 2-inch cleat extending downward at each end of the lid. The smooth top of such a lid can be covered with metal to increase its weather resistance. When making hive bodies, you have the option of dadoing the handholds into them, about 2 inches below the top, or nailing a ¾ × 2-inch cleat at the same level on each end of the hive bodies. It is much easier to handle heavy supers of honey by grasping such cleats instead of handholds. The hive bottom in the plan provides a ⅜-inch-deep entrance. If you prefer to make a deeper entrance, cut the spacer strips to the height you desire, such as ¾ or ⅞ inch. Bottoms with 2 × 2-inch rather than ¾ × 4-inch cleats make it a little easier to pick up the hive and may also help to keep the hive a little drier. The hive pattern can be adapted to make nuc boxes by narrowing the hive width to provide room for 3 or 5 frames rather than 10. To make pallets for use in

CONSTRUCTION DETAILS
10-FRAME BEE HIVE
(¾-inch-thick lumber)

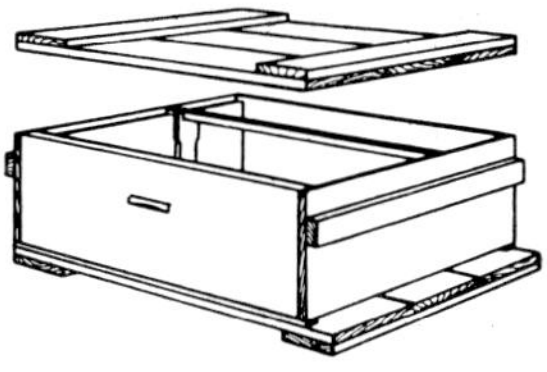

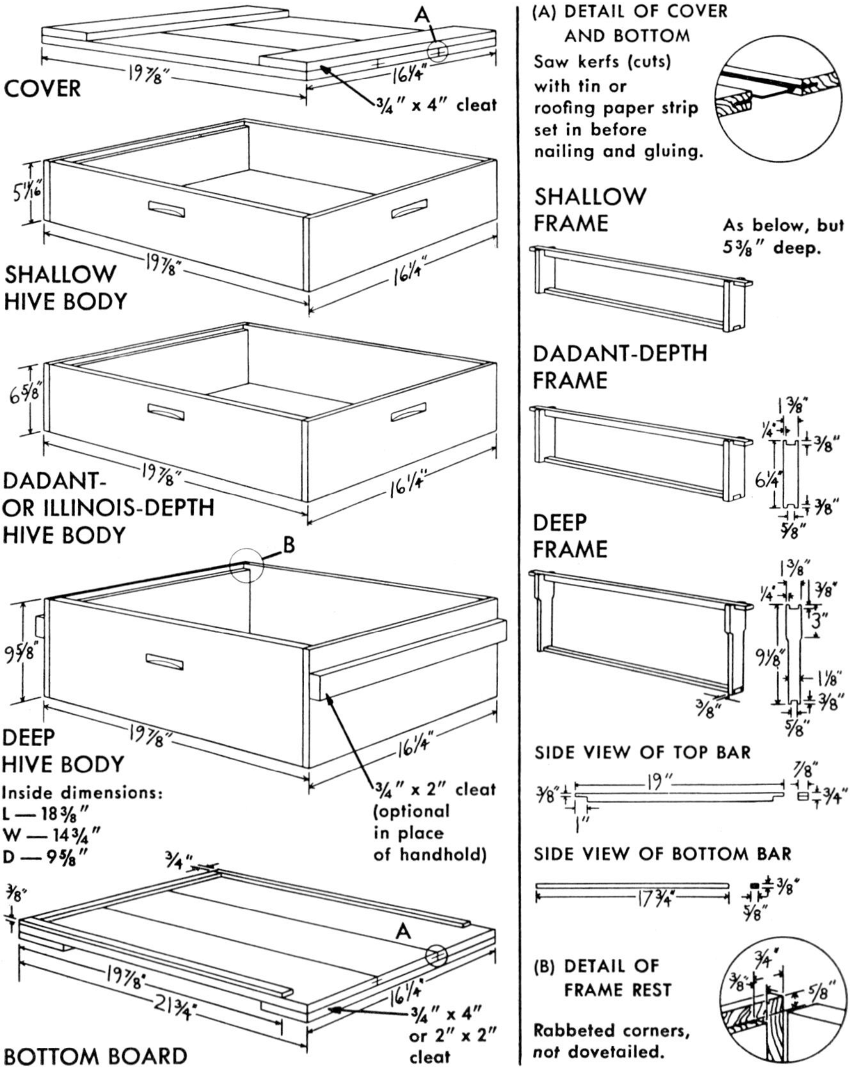

handling and storing stacks of hive bodies, follow the pattern for the hive cover and add a rim of spacer strips around the outer edge of the flat side of the lid. These will help to catch and confine honey and bits of wax that fall from combs.

Frame-making requires many saw cuts and can be dangerous without special equipment and techniques. It is usually better to buy frames than to risk a serious accident. However, if you decide to make them, use the pattern for frames with straight-sided end bars. These are easier to cut out and are as well accepted by the bees as frames with tapered or indented end bars.

Paint the hive bodies and lids on all surfaces, inside and out. This reduces the loss of paint by peeling and is not detrimental to the bees. Bottoms can be painted after being treated with wood preservative or, preferably, sealed with a couple coats of boiled linseed oil. Frames do not need any preservative treatment.

Making and using a frame-wiring board. A frame-wiring board is used to install horizontal wires in frames. These tightly drawn wires serve as supports for comb foundation and the comb constructed from it. The board is basically a jig in which a frame can be held firmly with the end bars or bottom bar under tension while special frame wire is threaded into place. A well-designed wiring board should make it relatively easy to thread the wire, to tighten it in the frame, and to fasten it in place. Releasing the frame from the board should further tighten the wire in the frame.

As seen in the construction plan on page 40, the base of the wiring board is a piece of ¾-inch-thick plywood. Beneath it are three cleats also of the same or similar lumber. Two cleats extend beyond the edges of the board and are drilled so that the board can be fastened firmly in place while it is being used. The L-shaped blocks at the front of the board are spaced so that the inside corners of the L's are 19 inches apart. They hold the frame top bar. The bottom bar fits into the wooden channel at the rear of the board. The channel has blocks at each end, 17¾ inches apart, to keep the frame from moving laterally. The overhanging lip of the channel, 1½ inches above the board, keeps the bottom bar from moving upward. There is a thin strip of wood approximately ⅛ inch thick and 1½ inches wide on the base board between the end blocks. This piece levels the frame in the jig.

In the center of the board is a clamping device made of ½ × ⅛-inch strap iron. The device consists of two arms riveted to a central lever that is bolted to the board. The rivets are centered ⅝ inch from the center of the bolt. The rear arm is about 9 inches long, the front one

CONSTRUCTION DETAILS
WIRING BOARD

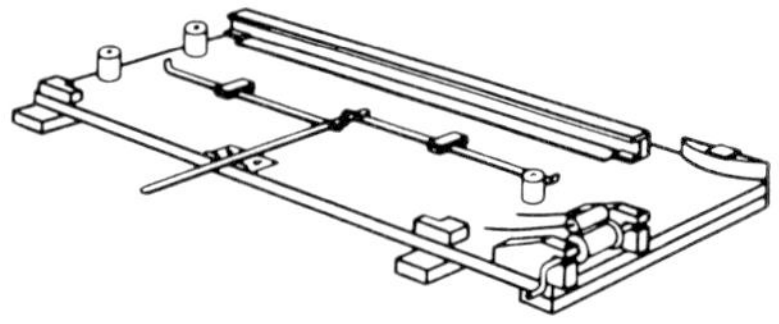

WIRING BOARD

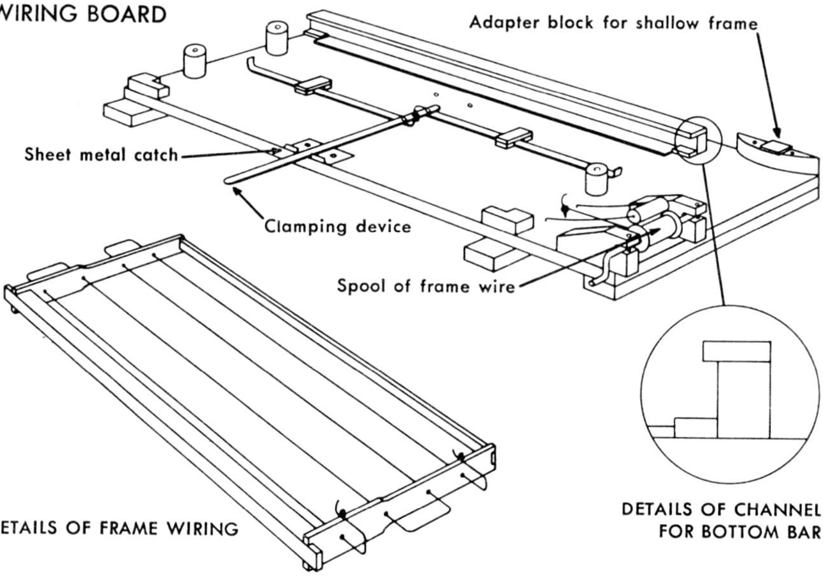

DETAILS OF FRAME WIRING

DETAILS OF CHANNEL FOR BOTTOM BAR

SIDE VIEW

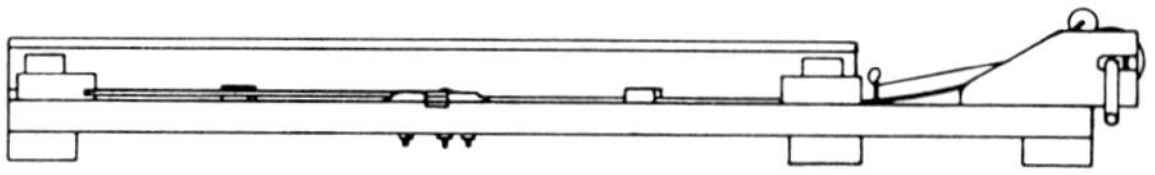

TOP VIEW

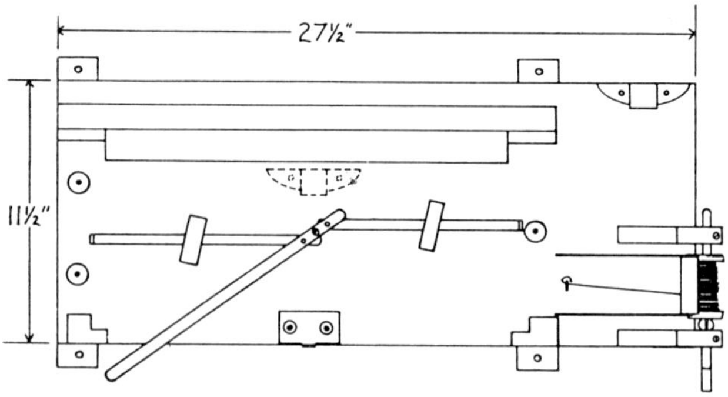

is 9½ inches, and each is bent upward an additional ½ inch. The central lever is about 12½ inches long. The arms slide through, but are kept in place by, wooden blocks near their midpoint. With the lever pulled to the left, the bent ends of the arms are far enough apart to accept a frame between them, about 17¾ inches wide. As the lever is moved to the right, the arms move inward, squeezing the end bars of the frame. A sheet metal catch attached to the base board holds the lever at the point where it exerts enough pressure to bend the end bars slightly inward but not so much that it damages the frame. The sheet metal catch has a ½-inch-wide notch in the center of a $^{3}/_{16}$-inch-wide vertical lip. This notch accepts and holds the clamping lever. The catch has elongated holes through which it is bolted to the base. It can be moved right or left to adjust the tension of the clamping lever. The clamping device is the most difficult part of the wiring board to make. It should be done last so that its size and location will fit the frame properly. The bolt that holds it to the base should be about midway between the frame ends and about 5½ inches from the front edge of the base.

The spool of frame wire is driven onto a splined crankshaft so that the wire can be held taut after it has been threaded through the frame. The shaft is supported and held in place by two wooden endpieces. A piece of wooden dowel on a sturdy-but-flexible, U-shaped wire keeps the frame wire from unreeling when it is not being used. The frame wire passes through a metal screw eye that puts it in line with the top hole in the end bar. When the wire is being threaded into a frame, it passes around three spools, or 1¼-inch lengths of 1-inch dowel or other wooden rod. The spools are located outside of, and ½ inch from, the frame end bars and are mounted so that they turn freely. Those on the left are centered between each pair of holes in the end bar. The one on the right is centered between the middle pair of holes.

The board is designed primarily for wiring full-depth (9⅛-inch) frames, but can be adapted for wiring Dadant-depth (6¼-inch) frames. In place of the metal clamping device, which will not fit the smaller frame, a special adapter block is used to hold and compress the shallower frame. The block can be seen in the drawing on the right rear corner of the board, where it is stored when not in use. The block is 1 inch high, 4¼ inches long, and 1 inch wide at the widest point of the curved edge. A 1⅛-inch-square piece of Masonite or other hardboard extends ⅛ inch beyond the curved side. This special block is mounted just to the rear of the metal clamping device, approximately in the location indicated by the dotted lines on the figure. The exact position must be determined by placing a 6¼-inch frame in place and marking the outside edge of the bottom bar. Fasten the curved edge of the block about 3/16 inch inside that line (toward the front of the board). The block will then press the bottom bar inward when the frame is pushed into place. When the frame is removed after being wired, the resiliency of the wood adds tension to the wire.

To wire a full-depth frame, place it on the board and fasten the metal clamp. Drive a wire nail into the upper edge of the right end bar just above the top and bottom holes. Leave the heads of the ¾-inch nails about ⅛ inch above the wood. Thread the wire through the top hole of each end bar, around the spool, and back across the frame. After threading it in this manner through all eight holes, wind the end of the wire tightly around the nail nearest the bottom bar, drive the nail in, and twist off the excess wire. Pull the wire off the spools and crank the excess back onto the spool of wire. Starting on the bottom section of wire where it is fastened, run your fingers along the wire, pulling it toward you. At the left end of the frame transfer your fingers quickly to the next section of wire, pulling the slack from it and from the lower wire. Follow this procedure on each wire while cranking excess wire back onto the spool. Try to get all wires tight enough to make a high note when plucked. You will have to learn how much pressure you can apply without breaking the wire. When you are satisfied with the amount of tension in the wire, grasp it just outside the end bar beneath the upper nail and wind the wire around the nail while keeping it tight in the frame. Drive in the nail and twist the wire to break it off. The same general system is also used for Dadant-depth frames.

Making equipment for embedding wires into comb foundation. Beeswax comb foundation, plain or wired, produces the strongest combs if it is installed in wired frames before it is given to a colony of bees. To be acceptable to the bees, the frame wires must be embedded in the wax of the foundation. The job of embedding can be done easily and quickly by using an electrical embedder and a special embedding board shown in the construction plan on the next page. The embedder heats the wire by briefly short-circuiting a 12-volt electrical current. The embedding board serves as a base on which to press the heated wires into the beeswax of the comb foundation.

The electrical embedder consists of a transformer, used to reduce house current to 12 volts, whose output wires are connected to copper contacts at either end of a ¾-inch-square piece of wood. There is only

CONSTRUCTION DETAILS
ELECTRICAL EMBEDDER & EMBEDDING BOARD

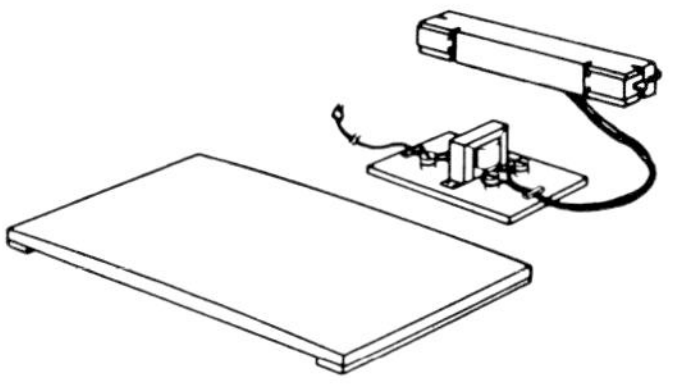

ELECTRICAL EMBEDDER

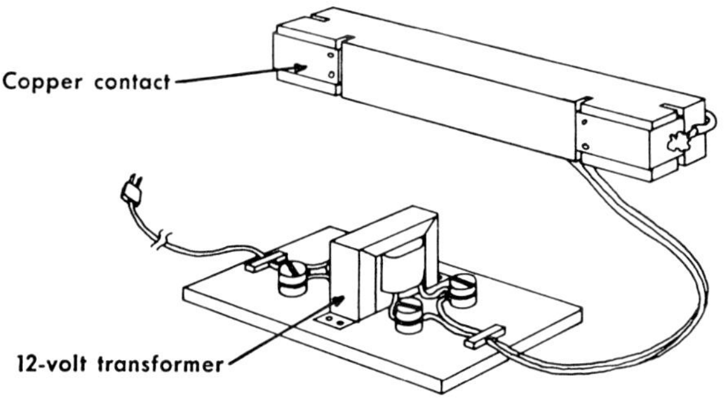

EMBEDDING BOARD

FOR FULL-DEPTH FRAME

For shallower frames, make board ¼" narrower than inside height.

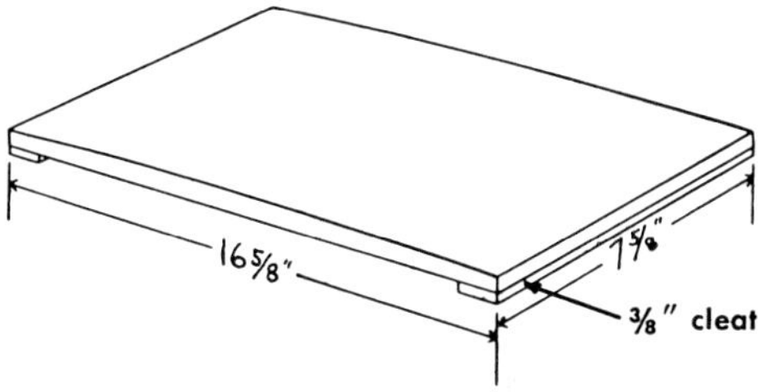

FRONT VIEW

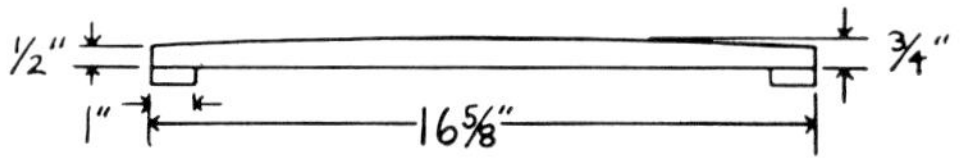

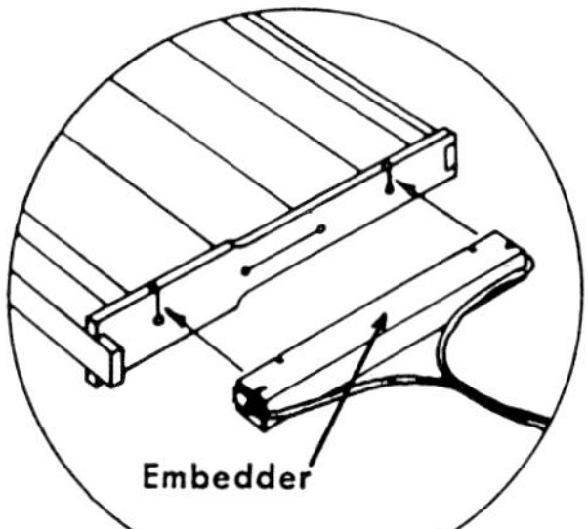

DETAILS OF END BAR WITH WIRES

one critical dimension in making such an embedder. The copper contacts must be spaced so that their centers are 6 inches apart for full-depth (9⅛-inch) frames and approximately 2 inches apart for shallow (6¼- and 5⅜-inch) frames. These contacts are pressed against the end portions of the wire that cross one end bar at right angles to it (see detail in construction plan). All the wire in the frame is heated at once when electrical contact is made.

The embedding board is a piece of ¾-inch-thick lumber cut to fit closely within the frames being used. It should be approximately 7⅝ × 16⅝ inches for full-depth frames, narrower for shallow frames. In order for the wires to make the best possible contact with the wax, the embedding board should have a convex curve on the longer dimension of its upper surface. From its ¾-inch thickness in the center, the board should taper to ½ inch at its outer ends. The cleats beneath the board provide needed additional height.

Place the frame on the embedding board with the comb foundation (already attached) beneath the wires. While pressing on the frame, contact the wires on the end bar with the embedder. Hold it in contact only briefly, a second or two at first, until you learn how much heat is needed to sink the wires into the foundation. Too long a contact will produce heat enough to cut plain foundation into strips or to melt wax away from the intersection of vertical and horizontal wires. Before embedding foundation, be sure it is warm, at least at room temperature. Afterwards, do not subject it to cold temperatures because the contraction and later expansion of the wax may cause the foundation to pull away from the wires.

Building a solar wax melter. A solar wax melter is a glass-covered box that uses the heat of the sun to melt beeswax and to separate it from honey and other materials with which it is found in honey bee colonies. The melter can be used to render old combs, cappings, burr comb, and other hive scrapings containing wax. It is also handy for removing beeswax from excluders. The melter produces wax of high quality and eliminates the need for the sometimes hazardous job of rendering wax in the home.

The sloping top surface of the solar wax melter provides maximum exposure to the sun and allows honey and melted wax to drain quickly into the storage pan. Before use, the entire unit, including the sheet-metal pan, should be painted black for maximum heat absorption. The glass cover with two sheets of double-strength glass about ¼ inch apart helps to retain the absorbed heat. The Celotex, or fiberboard, insulation also serves the same purpose. Internal temperatures well above the melting point of beeswax, about 145°F. (63°C.), are maintained on warm, sunny days. Place the melter in a sunny, sheltered spot for best results.

The plan on page 46 is meant to provide ideas on how to build a melter. It has been modified from one originally published by F. K. Böttcher of West Germany. You need not copy the plan exactly. For this reason, many dimensions are not given, especially the less important ones. A melter of the size illustrated will handle all the wax from up to 60 hives of bees. Modify the dimensions to fit your needs, or the materials available, but beware of making it too small. The sheet metal pan should be 4 to 6 inches deep and big enough to accept excluders (16¼ × 20 inches) or at least two full-depth frames (19 × 20 inches). Consider the possibility of making one or more cappings baskets of "expanded" metal that will fit into the sheet metal pan.

The pan to catch the hot honey and melted wax should be relatively large to prevent accidental overflows. The one illustrated is an inexpensive plastic dish pan readily available in many stores. The wax can be easily removed because it does not adhere well to the smooth, flexible plastic. The sloping sides of the pan also make it easier to remove the cake of wax.

The wooden brace is designed to support the lid while you clean out the slumgum, or residue, that remains after combs are melted. It lies between the exterior box and the interior layer of insulation. The finger hole, or notch, is used to pull it up into place. Cut the free end at an angle so that it makes firm contact with the lid frame when the lid is a suitable height to work beneath.

The melted wax will flow more easily down the pan if the combs, excluders, and cappings baskets are set on lengths of metal rods or angle iron. You should also put a coarse screen across the outlet of the pan to keep unmelted pieces of comb and other debris from flowing into the pan of molten wax. The honey collects beneath the wax in the pan. It is darkened and unsuitable for human food, but can be used to feed bees in early spring (*not* in the fall). The slumgum remaining in the sheet metal pan contains beeswax that can be removed only by a hot water press. If you accumulate 100 pounds or more, it is worthwhile having it rendered commercially.

The melter is highly attractive to robber bees because of the odors given off by the warm honey and wax. It should be kept tightly closed except when loading it or removing the filled collecting pan.

CONSTRUCTION DETAILS

SOLAR WAX MELTER

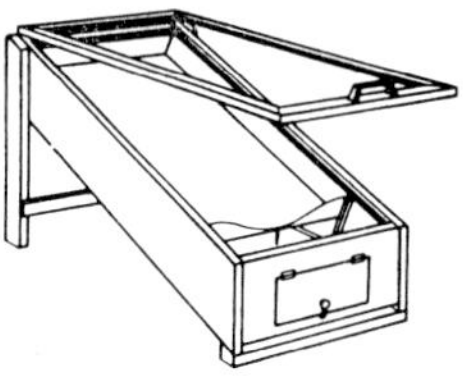

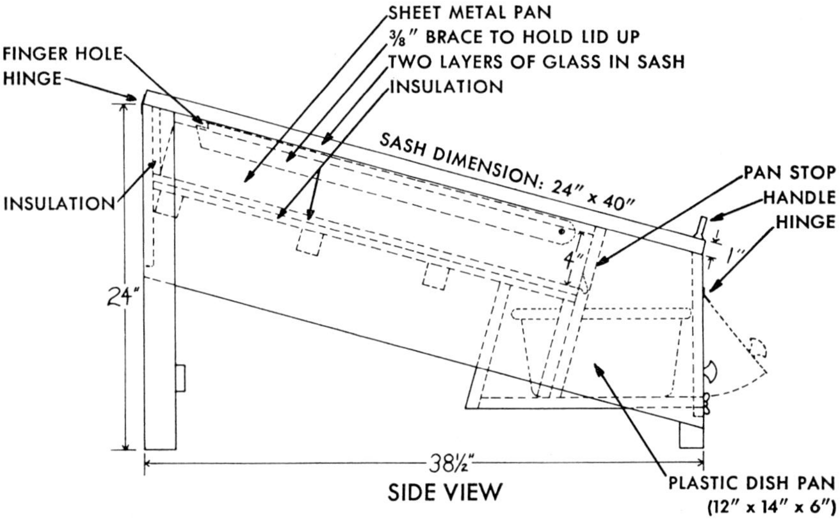

SIDE VIEW

The wax melter has a double layer of ½" Celotex, except for the top rear, which has a single layer, and the front, which has no insulation.

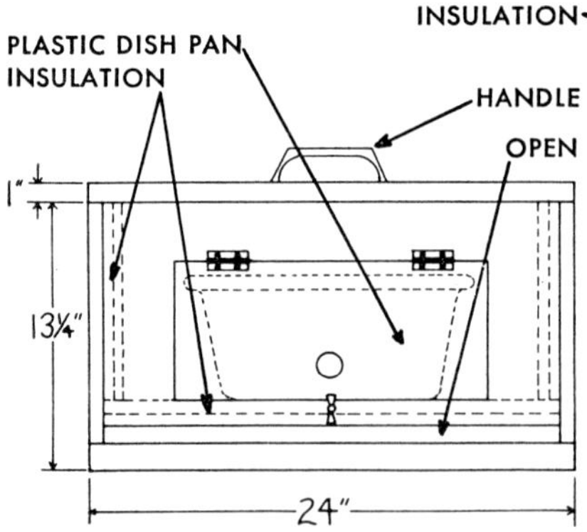

FRONT VIEW OF FACE

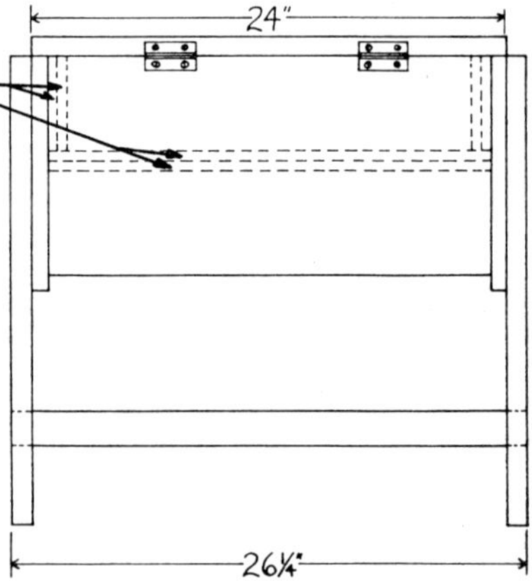

BACK VIEW

Making and using a pollen trap. A pollen trap is a device used by beekeepers to remove and collect pellets of pollen from the legs of honey bees as they return to the hive from foraging trips. The pollen is used to supplement the protein food of honey bee colonies in the spring, either by itself or in mixtures with materials such as soy flour and brewers' yeast. Pollen traps are also used by people interested in identifying and comparing the types and amounts of pollen collected by colonies of bees. Such studies indicate what plants are being visited and their relative importance in a particular area.

There are many types of pollen traps, but all operate in the same way. The bees entering the hive are forced to pass through two layers of 5-mesh hardware cloth with the holes offset and the screens about 1/4 inch apart. Traps are most effective in removing large loads of pollen, but they probably take only about 40 to 60 percent of the incoming loads, or pellets.

The pollen trap discussed here (see the construction plan on page 48) was originally designed at the Ontario Agricultural College in Canada and has been modified slightly to make it easier to construct and use. The design is a good one because it provides full ventilation for the colony and makes it easy to remove the collected pollen from the back of the hive without disturbing the colony.

In constructing the trap and interpreting the drawings, consider that the trap is composed of several layers, represented graphically by letters A through D on the left side of the plan. The bottom layer, D, is a standard bottom board of the type used in the eastern United States. It has been shortened to 19 7/8 inches, the same length as a hive body. The 7/8-inch-deep side is uppermost, and its opening faces the *rear* of the hive. The second layer, C, is the cloth-covered pollen tray onto which the pollen loads fall as they are pushed off the legs of bees passing through the two pollen-removing screens. The three long pieces of the pollen tray are 3/4-inch-square pine lumber. One crosspiece is 3/8 inch square; the other, 3/8 × 3/4 inch to give more space for the nails driven into it to hold the metal flashing. The flashing helps to keep rainwater out of the back of the trap. The unbleached muslin, or some other loosely woven cloth, should be stretched tightly and stapled to the top surface of the tray. It allows air to circulate through and around the pellets of pollen and helps to prevent mold growth.

The trap base, layer B, is really two layers as seen in the expanded view on the right. The lower portion is a U-shaped frame of 3/4-inch-square pine lumber on which a 16 1/4 × 19 7/8-inch piece of 8-mesh hardware cloth is stapled. The lack of a crosspiece at the rear of the trap allows additional space to remove the pollen tray when it is heavily

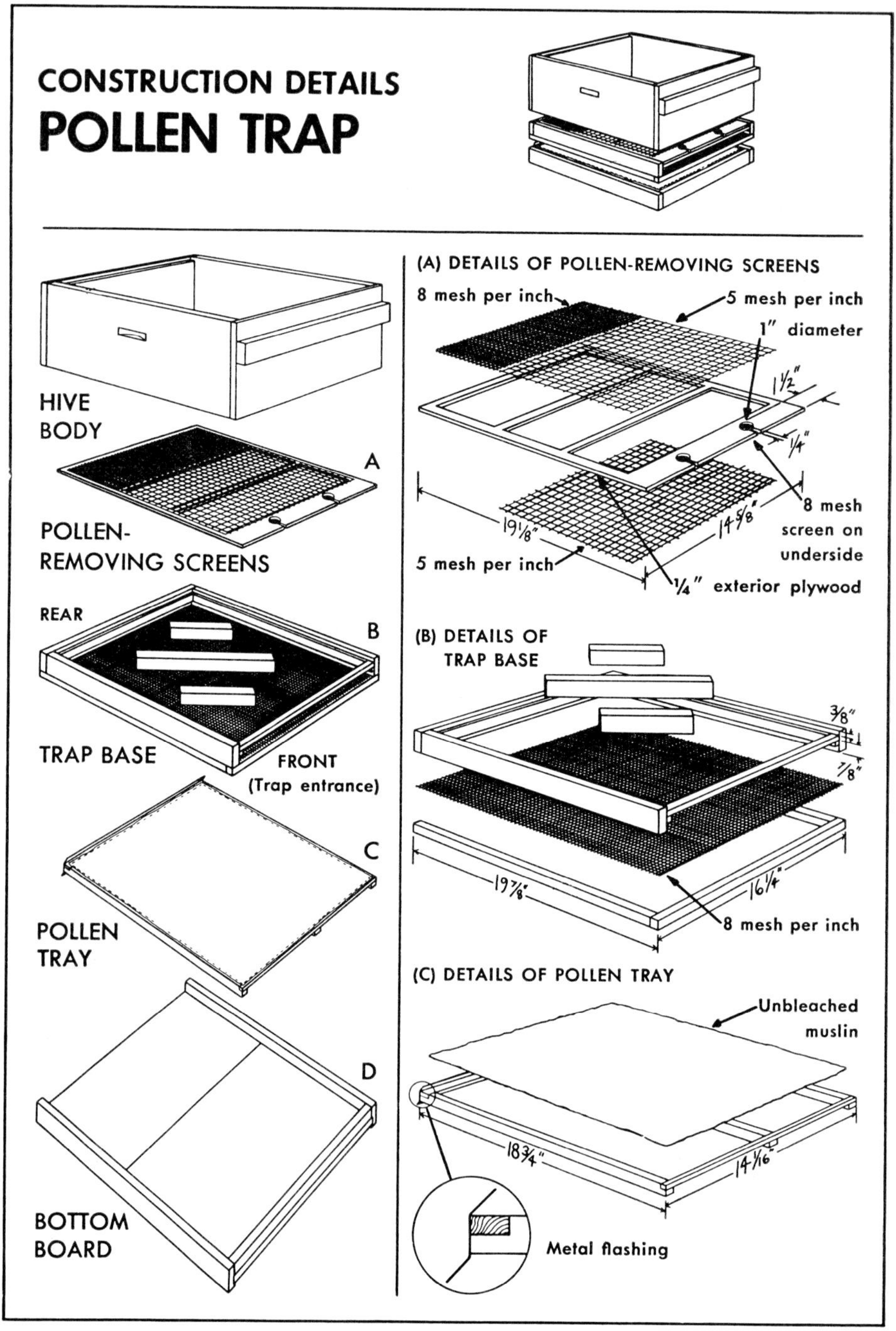
CONSTRUCTION DETAILS
POLLEN TRAP
HIVE BODY
A
POLLEN-REMOVING SCREENS
REAR
B
TRAP BASE
FRONT (Trap entrance)
C
POLLEN TRAY
D
BOTTOM BOARD
(A) DETAILS OF POLLEN-REMOVING SCREENS
8 mesh per inch
5 mesh per inch
1" diameter
1 1/2"
1/4"
8 mesh screen on underside
19 1/8"
14 5/8"
5 mesh per inch
1/4" exterior plywood
(B) DETAILS OF TRAP BASE
3/8"
7/8"
19 7/8"
16 1/4"
8 mesh per inch
(C) DETAILS OF POLLEN TRAY
Unbleached muslin
18 3/4"
14 1/16"
Metal flashing

covered with pollen pellets. Three pieces of ¾-inch pine lumber are placed diagonally on the hardware cloth and stapled to it from below. One piece is 14 inches long, and the shorter two are 8 inches long. All are 1½ inches high. These allow bees to move more easily through the pollen-removing screens, and they help to distribute the pollen more evenly on the pollen tray.

The upper portion of the trap base is a U-shaped frame of ¾-inch pine lumber 2 inches high. There is a framework of ⅜ × ¾-inch cleats fastened ⅜ inch below the top. This framework supports the pollen-removing screens. The front cleat is oriented so that its narrow side faces the entrance, thus making the entrance as deep as possible. The entrance opening is 1⁵⁄₁₆ inches high and 14¾ inches wide. The two portions of the trap base are nailed together as in illustration B.

The pollen-removing screens, layer A, are fastened to a framework of ¼-inch exterior plywood or other wood of the same thickness. In the rim at the front of this frame are two 1-inch holes with ⁵⁄₁₆-inch-wide channels leading to the front edge. The holes and channels are covered underneath with 8-mesh hardware cloth. These allow drones to get out of the hive. They cannot pass through the pollen-removing screens, and their dead bodies can clog the screens.

The pollen-removing screens are two layers of 5-mesh hardware cloth with their holes offset. The rear section, where few bees attempt to pass, is covered with one layer of 8-mesh hardware cloth for additional ventilation. Five-mesh hardware cloth is not generally available, but can be purchased from bee supply companies.

All wooden parts of the trap should be painted or varnished to resist the weather.

Put the trap on during periods when the bees are actively collecting pollen. You can expect to collect ¼ to 1 pound per day per trap, depending on the colony's activity and the sources of pollen available. Since the trap takes only part of the pollen from the bees, it can be left on for periods of several weeks without damaging the colony. However, because honey production can be reduced somewhat, you may wish to trap pollen for one to three weeks and then remove the screens for an equal period before collecting pollen again from the same colony.

Pollen should be removed from the trap at least every two or three days. Put it in plastic bags and store it a 0°F. (−18°C.) until used.

All pollen traps are vulnerable to water damage to the pollen, and this one is no exception. Wind-driven rain entering the front or back of the trap may wet the pollen on the cloth-covered tray. To reduce such losses you may need to devise a storm hood that shelters the entrance without hindering the bees when entering the hive.

Ants are a common pest in pollen traps. Use oil pans or sticky barriers to keep them out. Do not use insecticides of any kind or you may also kill the bees.

Occasionally you will find a colony that does not adjust to the presence of a pollen trap on its hive. The bees will cluster at the hive entrance and within the trap long after other colonies have adapted to it. When you find such a colony, it is best to remove the trap to another colony because otherwise your pollen yield will be quite low.

Making a bee veil. Bee veils of black nylon net are easy to make and have several advantages. When rolled up, they fit easily into a shirt pocket or glove compartment. They are easy to see through and are cooler than other types of veils. Their disadvantages include ease of snagging, melting if touched by flame or spark, and touching the face or neck in a wind.

Suitable, 72-inch-wide net material is available at most fabric stores. The sketch on the next page shows the desirable mesh size. It must be black so that you can see through it well. Other colors, especially the light ones, cannot be used.

Make a paper pattern the size indicated in the sketch. This size is suitable for a tall person and a large-brimmed hat. The veil circumference can be adjusted to fit around the brim of the hat on which it will be worn. The top elastic should fit snugly around the hat's crown. After making one veil, you may wish to adjust other measurements to fit the individual who wears the veil. The back should always be shorter than the front to help keep the net from touching the neck. A large hat brim also helps in this regard.

Place the paper pattern on the folded net with the front of the pattern along the fold. After cutting it out, sew the back of the veil with a flat-felled or French seam. Make a casing around the top of the veil to hold the elastic. Make another casing around the bottom except for a 6-inch section at the center front. Put the elastic into the bottom casing. Attach the center 6 inches of the nylon cord to the front of the veil with black bias tape or seam tape. At the same time lap the ends of the elastic around the cord before it is sewn beneath the tape. This is the most difficult and important part of the job. The net, tape, cord, and elastic must be attached firmly together or you will quickly get holes at each end of the tape. The final step is to put elastic in the casing at the top of the veil and sew its ends together.

When you put the veil on, pull the front down so that the elastic is stretched against your chest. Loop the cord ends around your body in opposite directions, bring them back in front, and tie them together.

CONSTRUCTION DETAILS
NYLON NET BEE VEIL

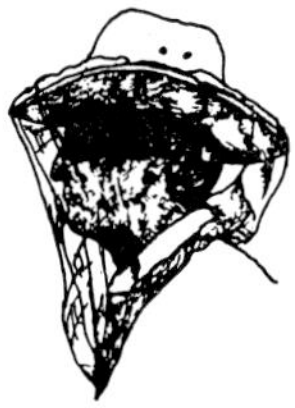

PAPER PATTERN

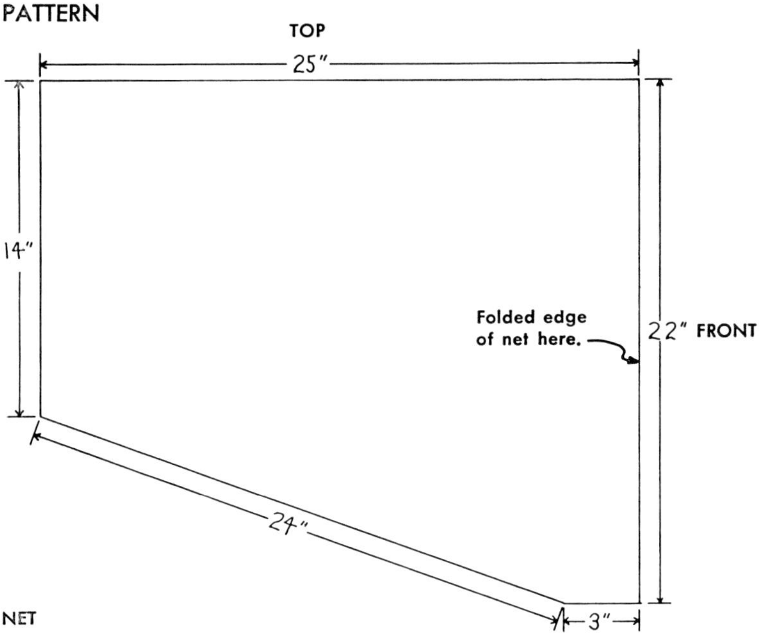

NYLON NET

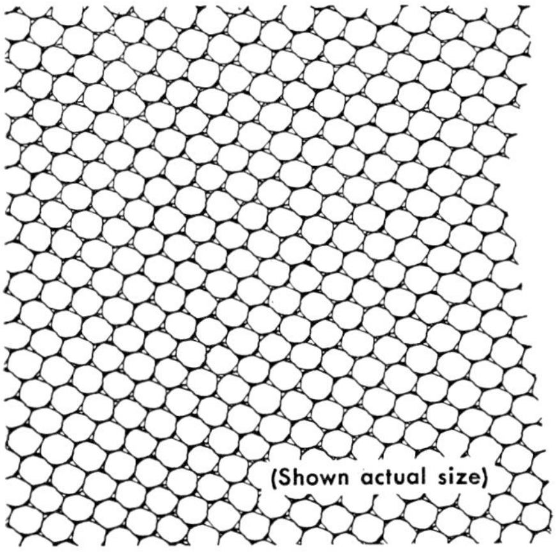

MATERIALS NEEDED

NYLON NET, 72" WIDE — 22"

BLACK ELASTIC, ¼" WIDE — 53"
23" for the top
30" for the bottom

BLACK BIAS TAPE
OR SEAM TAPE — 6"

NYLON CORD — 8'

Measurements include allowances for seams and casings.

SPRING MANAGEMENT: STARTING WITH BEES

When and How to Start

Spring is the ideal time to begin keeping bees. In the Midwest the best months for this are April and May, depending on the state or location, and when fruit trees, dandelions, and early flowers are in bloom. The reasons for starting at this time are that the spring blossoms and the lengthening days help to get the bees off to a good start and the early start allows the colony to increase its population in time to store honey from the clovers and other major food sources that begin to yield nectar usually in June, but varying widely.

Established colonies. A beginning beekeeper should start with at least two colonies but not more than four or five. With more than one colony you have the advantage of being able to exchange brood, bees, and combs in case one of the colonies needs some help. With too many colonies you may have only enough time to keep them supplied with supers, and not be able to enjoy learning the details of the activities in any of them. The beginner can purchase established colonies from a local beekeeper but should do so with care. Hives offered for sale may be homemade, with poor combs and, sometimes, the bees may be diseased. There is nothing wrong with good homemade equipment built to proper dimensions, but hive bodies and frames made without regard for the proper bee space are worthless. The amount of honey in the hive that you buy is not as important as the quality of the equipment as long the there is at least a small reserve supply. The bees themselves can be improved at slight expense by requeening the colony. Buy established colonies only after they have been inspected and found free of disease by a qualified apiary inspector. Such inspections are usually available on request from your state Department of Agriculture.

If you buy full-sized colonies, you will lose the opportunity to watch the fascinating early development of the colony that you have if you buy package bees or small "nucleus" colonies of three to five frames. Also, newly established small colonies are easier for the beginner to observe and manipulate than are the larger ones. In part, this is because of the beginner's reaction to the number of bees present and also because of the greater number of guard bees and field bees in the larger colony. They are not necessarily meaner, but more bees react when large colonies are handled. Consider this difference when you begin keeping bees because it is essential that you open the hive regularly and learn about the inside activities of the colony.

Package bees. Package bees (Fig. 25) consist of 2 to 4 pounds of bees and a laying queen shipped in a screened cage with a can of sugar syrup to provide food en route. They are produced in commercial apiaries in the southeastern United States and in California. Order them early, in January if possible, in order to have the best chance of receiving them on time, preferably during early fruit and dandelion bloom in your area. A 2-pound package with a queen will produce as good a colony as a 3-pound package if it is fed well and gets off to a good, early start on drawn combs. However, for installation on foundation, a 3-pounder is usually a better choice. Packages hived on frames filled with foundation must be fed continually with sugar syrup until their combs are completed and there is stored honey in the combs. This may require a month or more if nectar is not available because of lack of bloom or poor spring weather. The food is a good investment because it is used to produce wax for comb building and to feed developing young bees. Any excess is stored for future use in the colony. Without such food the bees may fail to build comb and may die. Use syrup

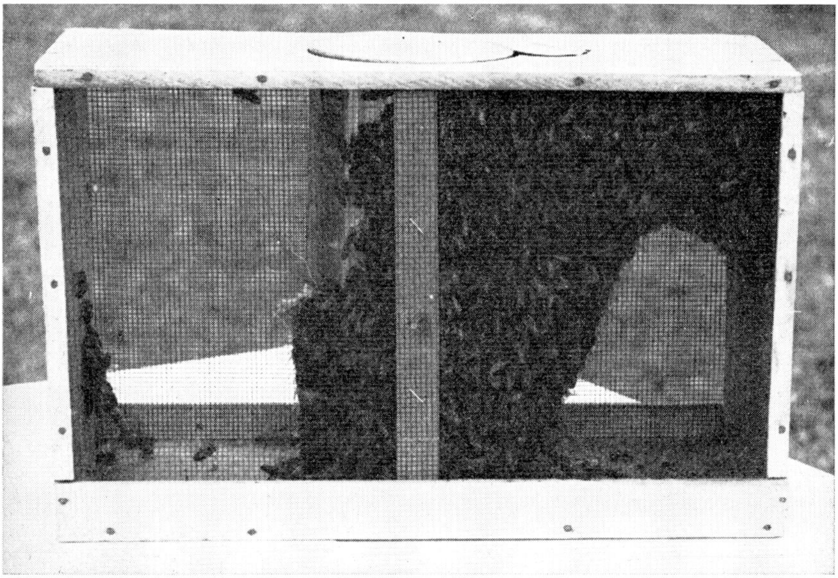

A 2-pound package of bees. **(Fig. 25)**

made from two volumes of granulated, white beet or cane sugar dissolved in one volume of hot water. This ratio of sugar to water is used most economically by the bees. However, thinner syrup of equal volumes of sugar and water can also be used. A gallon can or large jar placed above the brood nest makes a better feeder than the entrance type (see page 104). The colony will reduce its intake or refuse syrup altogether when nectar becomes readily available to them. Wash and exchange feeders regularly so that the syrup does not become fermented or contaminated by the growth of fungus or other organisms.

Package bee colonies develop more rapidly when installed on combs containing honey and pollen. They can be started a little earlier in the season because of the pollen that is available immediately for rearing brood. The beginner usually has no choice but to start with foundation the first year. In subsequent years, however, install packages on combs if at all possible.

Package bees usually are shipped with instructions for placing them in the hive. The bees are not difficult to handle if you remember some important fundamental details. A complete one-story hive must be ready to accept the bees and a location must have been chosen for it. When the package arrives, put it in a dark, cool place such as a basement until you can install the bees in the hive, preferably the same day. If you must delay the job, check to see that there is still syrup in the feeder can in the package. With plenty of food the bees can be kept in the package for a day or two if necessary. Late afternoon or evening is the best time to install them so that the bees will settle down quickly without flying very much. When you are ready to start, place the cage on its side and spray, sprinkle, or brush warm sugar syrup on the side of the screened cage. Use only as much syrup as the bees will clean up readily. Do not soak them with it. When the bees are gorged with syrup they are gentler and less inclined to fly and sting.

When you are ready to install the bees, put on your veil, get your hive tool, and place the hive on location with five frames set to one side of it. A smoker is rarely needed but you should have it ready. Also have the cover and the equipment ready to feed the bees after they are installed. Stuff the hive entrance lightly with green grass or reduce its size with an entrance cleat. Loosen the cover of the package but do not remove it. The queen cage is usually beside the syrup can at the top of the package or hanging by a wire or tin strip below the can. Give the package a sharp bounce on the ground to knock the bees to the floor. Remove the syrup can and queen cage and replace the cover over the hole. Expose the white candy in the queen cage by removing the cork or other covering from the small hole in the candy-filled end of the cage.

Then wedge the cage, candy-end up, between two frames in the center of the frames in the hive. Bounce the cage again and pour the bees into the empty space in the hive, shaking the cage back and forth to dislodge the bees and to get them out of the cage (Fig. 26). You may have to repeat this procedure several times until no more bees will come out. Leave the cage beside the hive entrance overnight with the hole beside the entrance and touching the bottom board. If the queen cage contains only a queen and no candy, or if you want to use the fast-release method, shake the bees into the box as described above. Then sprinkle syrup on the queen cage to wet the queen and prevent her from flying. Hold the queen cage down in the hive, remove the screen, and drop the queen among the bees. When the queen is in, quickly but gently replace the frames in the hive and put the feeder in place. Whatever method you use to introduce the queen, leave the hive alone for at least 5 days, except to refill the feeder if needed. Then, on a warm afternoon, take a brief look at the colony. Use only a little smoke and handle the bees and equipment gently. Look primarily for eggs and larvae that indicate the queen has been accepted and is laying. Remove the queen cage after checking it to be sure it no longer contains the queen. Close the hive quietly after checking the syrup supply. Any colony without a queen should be given another one without delay to avoid losing the entire colony.

Nucleus colonies. Another way to start is to purchase a nucleus, a complete small colony. A nucleus, with three to five frames of brood, bees, and a queen, compares in price with package bees and has the advantage of having developing bees that will quickly increase the size of the colony. In purchasing nuclei locally, be sure they are from colonies that have been inspected for disease. Nuclei may carry a flat price or, sometimes, a lower price that requires an exchange of an equal number of frames of foundation. The frames of brood and bees can be placed into your prepared equipment. The colony will need incoming nectar or sugar syrup until all its combs are completed. (See page 25 or page 103.)

Other sources of bees. Honey bee colonies, together with their combs, can be transferred from a tree or house into a modern hive. However, because of the amount of work involved and the difficulty of obtaining good combs, you should avoid this method of obtaining bees unless you have no alternative. Swarms also can be used to establish your first colony or to provide additional new colonies for your apiary. They are not usually available as early in the season as package bees, which are more suitable for an early spring start. Most swarms contain old queens that should be replaced during the summer.

Shaking a package of bees into the hive. (Fig. 26)

Location and Arrangement of Colonies

The location and arrangement of an apiary is important to the bees, to the owner of the bees, and to the people and animals close-by. Bees are affected by the exposure of the hive in relation to wind, sun, and the surface on which the hive is placed. Protecting hives from prevailing winds, especially in winter, will result in stronger colonies. Hives should be located so that the sun hits them at least in the morning and early afternoon. In the Midwest, colonies are rarely damaged by being in full sun, but afternoon shade is beneficial. With shaded hives, the bees may forage better because fewer bees are required to cool the hive and to carry water for evaporation. Reflected heat from around the hive also affects the colony. Grass or other ground covers reflect less heat than exposed soil. Asphalt areas or tarred roofs are not suitable sites for hives. Never place colonies in low areas subject to flooding or where water stands after heavy rains.

Traditionally, hives in apiaries have always been arranged in straight rows. It is much better to place the hives in some irregular pattern so that field bees are more likely to return to their own colonies. With hives in a straight row, foragers drift to the end hives and increase their populations at the expense of the colonies in the center of the rows. For convenience, the hives can be arranged in pairs about 6 inches apart. Pairs of hives can be separated from one another by several feet. A semicircle or U-shaped arrangement reduces drifting and makes it easy to handle the colonies with a hive loader.

Flowering plants within about a mile of the colony are important to its success. A good apiary location should have spring nectar and pollen plants as well as plants that provide the main nectar source later in the year. Ornamental trees and shrubs provide early pollen and nectar for bees in or near cities and towns. As a result the colonies develop faster than in areas of open framland. Later in the season a farm-based colony may have the advantage of more clovers and other crops that produce nectar. Remember this difference if you have to choose between two locations. Also consider the possibility of moving hives to take advantage of different areas with more available nectar and pollen plants. There is a saying that good locations make good beekeepers. Commercial beekeepers must seek and test new locations regularly (Fig. 27).

When locating the hives, you also need to consider the conditions under which you will have to work with the bees. Just keeping the bees in a sunny spot will help because they will be easier to handle if the colony is warm and flying well. Don't put hives under a tree or in similar spots where you cannot stand comfortably to open them. Since you will manipulate the hives from the side, leave space on at least one side for standing and for handling equipment. You will enjoy the bees most if you look within the hive regularly — at least weekly in good weather. For this reason, keep hives as close to home as possible where you can observe them readily. Obviously, not everyone can keep several colonies in the backyard, but you are more likely to find the time to master them if they are close-by.

A final consideration in locating your colony is an important one. Bees can be a nuisance in several ways wherever they are kept. However, you can reduce or prevent problems by planning ahead. Bees are liable to sting people and animals in the vicinity of their hive and in the flight path between it and the plants they visit. To offset this tendency, try to screen the hive or apiary to make the bees fly above the heads of passersby. Bees also spot cars, clothing, and buildings in the vicinity of the hive by releasing their body wastes in flight. Spotting from a single colony is not serious but several colonies flying largely in one direction may make a car or a house unsightly in a short time. When nectar is not available bees cause problems by visiting sources of water such as water faucets, children's wading pools, and bird baths.

An excellent apiary location. (Fig. 27)

Once they become accustomed to a watering place, they will continue to use it all during the flying season. Water must always be available close to the hives, starting the day a colony is established or moved. Provide a tank or pan with something in it on which the bees can land. Cork floats or crushed rock can be used for this purpose. A hose or faucet dripping onto a board or cement slab is also suitable.

Handling the Colony

The beginner with bees is naturally reluctant at first to spend much time looking at the colony within the hive and is usually a little over-cautious about handling the bees and about damaging the colony. With proper clothing and equipment there is no reason to hesitate. And don't worry about the colony — it can be damaged far more by neglect than by too much attention.

If you have been stung by a bee without more effect than the usual swelling, you have little to worry about in handling a colony. A few people, however, react strongly to bee stings and may have trouble breathing; they may even go into shock or unconsciousness. When this happens the person should be taken immediately to a doctor for treatment with adrenalin (epinephrine). The effect of a bee sting can be reduced by promptly removing the sting. Scrape it off, being careful not to squeeze it and drive additional venom into the skin. When you are stung while handling bees, quickly remove the sting and smoke the spot. The smoke repels bees and covers the odor of the sting that otherwise may attract bees to sting the same spot. It is also a good idea to smoke your hands, gloves, and ankles before you begin handling a colony.

Before opening a hive, you need to light the smoker. It is essentially a firebox with a grate and a bellows. To work properly and to provide thick, cool smoke it must have coals above the grate and unburned material above them. A burlap sack cut into strips makes good smoker fuel. Rotten or pitchy wood, corn cobs, and shavings are also suitable. Light a small quantity of fuel and puff the bellows until the material flames. Add more pieces, while puffing the bellows, until the barrel of the smoker is full but not packed tightly. Once started well, a smoker will not go out when you need it. Refill it and pack it down with your hive tool as you work. Keep the smoke cool and thick.

After putting on your veil, approach the hive from the rear and work from either side. If several colonies or rows of colonies face the same direction, examine the front hive or row first so that you later work behind the disturbed colonies. Avoid jarring the hive or setting the smoker on it before opening the hive. Blow several puffs of smoke into the hive entrance and into any other hive openings such as auger holes or large cracks through which bees can crawl. The smoke repels and distracts the guard bees. Pry the cover up slowly with the hive tool, hold the edge up 2 or 3 inches, and blow several good puffs of smoke beneath it. With too much smoke you can make bees run and "boil" out of the hive. But it is better to use plenty of smoke, even too much, while you are learning to handle bees, than to use too little. You will soon learn to gauge how much is needed by observing the actions of the bees. On warm days when a nectar flow is in progress, you need very little smoke. More smoke than usual is needed in cool and cloudy weather.

Once the cover or a hive body is lifted, remove it without letting it back down in place. In this way you crush fewer bees and alarm the colony less. Place the cover, underside up, on the ground close beside you toward the rear of the hive. In this position it serves as a place to put the second story when you look at the bottom brood chamber of a two-story hive (Fig. 28). If you want to look at both hive bodies, separate them, using smoke, and look at the lower one first. Otherwise many bees move to the lower body and make it harder for you to examine the combs. Smoke the bees in the top hive body before you put it back on the lower one.

Examining a two-story colony of bees. The top shallow super is placed on the inverted cover at the rear of the hive. (Fig. 28)

With the cover off, you should be able to see the area with the greatest number of bees, especially in a package colony or nucleus. This area is the brood nest where the queen and developing bees are located. To look at the colony, you must first loosen and remove a frame at the edge of the brood nest or, in large colonies, the first or second frame from the edge of the hive. Pry the frames apart with the straight end of the hive tool. New frames separate easily, but you may have to force older ones apart at the end bars in order to break the bits of comb and propolis holding them.

Pull the first frame slowly out of the hive, look briefly for the queen and, if she is not on the frame, set it on end against the opposite side of the hive near the entrance. If the queen is on the frame, it is better not to set the frame outside the hive where she may fall on the ground. The rest of the frames can then be examined and replaced in order. Hold the combs above the colony when looking at them, with the comb surface vertical (Fig. 29). Pollen and nectar may fall from combs held horizontally. To look at the opposite side of a comb, raise or lower one end until the top bar is vertical. Pivot the frame 180 degrees and bring the top bar back to a horizontal position. Repeat the process before replacing the comb in the hive. Put the first frame back in its original position.

One application of smoke usually lasts for several minutes. Then you may notice bees lining up along the tops of the frames looking at you. Before they decide to fly at you, give them a puff or two of smoke to drive them back down. To close the hive, smoke the bees at the top of the hive, strike the cover on the ground in front of the colony to knock off adhering bees, and lower the cover slowly into place. When putting any equipment with bees in it back together, pause slightly just before the parts touch; most of the bees will move out of the way.

The standard hive holds 10 frames with a little extra space when they are new. In a short time, additional wax and propolis make it difficult to remove the individual frames. For this reason, commercial and amateur beekeepers commonly violate the bee-space concept and use 9 frames evenly spaced in each hive body, in brood chambers as well as in honey supers. To obtain the best possible combs, you should use full hive bodies of foundation that contain 10 frames. When using mixtures of drawn comb and foundation, you may space 9 frames

Holding brood comb in a vertical position. **(Fig. 29)**

evenly or push them together in the center of the hive. In the latter case the frames should be spaced evenly after the bees begin to use the foundation but before they build extra comb in the spaces next to the outer frames.

Colonies of bees may make better combs and survive the winter better when they have 10 frames in each brood chamber. However, before deciding on one system of management, you should test both systems in your own apiary to see which best suits both you and the bees.

What to Look for in the Colony

Above all, most beekeepers want to see the queen bee in the colony. Finding her is usually easier in a small colony than in a large one. In either case, she is sometimes elusive and may be found on the wall of the hive or on the bottom board instead of on the combs. You can find the queen most easily by smoking the colony lightly and looking quickly at all the combs within the brood nest. She is often found on a comb containing eggs, or on one with the cells that have been cleaned and are ready to receive eggs. The quality of the queen can be judged without seeing her by the pattern in which she lays her eggs in the comb. Large solid areas of sealed brood, and concentric rings of eggs and larvae of different ages are the signs of a good queen. It takes practice to recognize eggs and young larvae at the base of the cells; learn to identify them readily. (See Figure 30.) Shake the bees off a frame into the hive in order to see details in the comb more easily. You can make the bees move away from an area of comb by touching them lightly on their backs with your finger or the flat end of a hive tool.

The brood pattern should be solid, with few open or unused cells (Fig. 31). A spotted pattern may indicate that the queen had a sex allele the same as one or more of the drones with which she mated. Such a queen should be replaced. The egg-laying behavior of the queen may produce a spotted brood pattern when she does not fill all the adjoining cells with eggs. She also should be replaced. Brood diseases kill larvae and pupae and create an uneven, spotted appearance of the brood combs. As explained in the section on diseases, you must learn to detect diseases or, at least, to recognize abnormal larvae and pupae. (See page 133.) By doing so, you will know when to ask for help in identifying the disease, or you may be able to diagnose it yourself by comparing the symptoms with the descriptions of brood diseases. Proper diagnosis and control of disease, especially American foulbrood, is extremely important. Otherwise you may lose all your bees and spread infection to other colonies within flight range of your apiary.

Eggs in new worker comb are shown at the top, and mature worker larvae nearly ready to be sealed in their cells are shown in the center. The bottom illustration shows worker pupae with their eyes colored; the cell cappings have been removed to expose the developing bees. (Fig. 30)

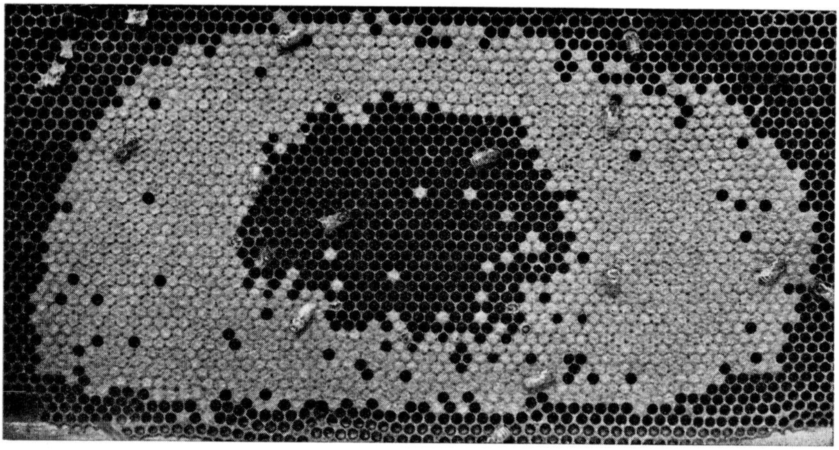

A comb from the brood nest showing a good pattern of sealed brood. Young bees have emerged from the center cells. The queen will lay eggs in the center cells as soon as they have been cleaned and polished. (Fig. 31)

The brood nest of the colony is an ellipsoidal or spherical area within the frames. The comb in the center of the brood nest has a large area of brood on each side. The combs toward the outer edges of the nest have smaller and smaller brood areas until the ones on the edge of the nest have only pollen and honey without brood. It is important to keep these combs (frames) in order in a small colony, especially when the temperature may go below 57°F. (14°C.), the clustering temperature of a colony. If you put a large frame of brood near the edge of the cluster, the bees may not be able to keep it covered and warm because the shape of the brood nest has been changed. Eggs and developing bees can be injured or killed by being chilled. In large colonies, and during warm weather, the order of the combs is not as important. However, it is best to keep brood combs together, with combs of pollen and honey on the edges and above the brood nest.

The colony needs pollen and honey in the hive all year as food for the adults and for rearing young bees. It has been estimated that a full cell of each type of food is needed to produce one young bee. The pollen supplies proteins, vitamins, and other minor nutrients. Honey provides carbohydrates in the form of several sugars. Honey removed from the hives must be only the *surplus* produced by the colony. If more than that is taken, or if it is taken at the wrong time, the bees may starve. A beekeeper must learn to estimate the amount of food, particularly honey, in the hive at each observation and to decide whether the colony is "making a living" or needs some help until more nectar is available. Learn to do this each time you open your hives, especially package colonies or any small colony just getting started. In early spring the bees may be unable to fly for a week or more because of cool or wet weather. At this time, and any time before the major nectar flow period, a colony needs 10 to 20 pounds of reserve food or the equivalent of two or three well-filled combs. You can test for incoming nectar in the hive by holding a comb flat above the open hive and giving it a quick shake downward. Any thin nectar in the comb will splash down onto the tops of the frames where it will be reclaimed by the bees.

When nectar is not available in the field, bees attempt to steal honey from other colonies. The guard bees of strong colonies attack and repel the robbers, but weaker colonies are sometimes overcome and killed by large numbers of robbing bees. The problem is most serious in the spring and the fall at any time hives are opened and combs exposed to bees. The natural defense system of the colony is disturbed by smoke and by the separation of the parts of the hive. Bees from other colonies are attracted and they fly around the exposed combs trying to get some of the colony's stored honey. Even after the hive is put back together, the robber bees may gather along the edges of the cover and other cracks in the hive. They will also try to get into the entrance of the colony as well as other nearby colonies. A beekeeper must learn to recognize the presence of robber bees and to take action to prevent the buildup of widespread robbing. This means keeping hives open only briefly when robbing is liable to occur and being careful not to expose combs, especially ones not protected by bees. It is easier to prevent robbing than to stop it. Always pick up bits of comb in the apiary and try not to let nectar or honey drip outside any hive. Robber bees can be recognized by their darting flight around combs and open hives, often with their legs hanging down. They land on combs and move quickly to cells of honey to fill up. If you see robbing starting, it is a good idea to stop looking at the bees and close the hive. As a precautionary measure, you can stuff grass or weeds lightly into the entrances to reduce their size. With small entrances to guard, the bees of a colony are better able to repel robbers.

The Need for Space in the Spring

The colony increases rapidly in size in April and May. It needs room for brood rearing, for storing honey and pollen, and for the increasing number of adult bees. Since one of the primary causes of swarming is crowding of adult bees, the colony should have two or more full-depth hive bodies or their equivalent to reduce the chance of early swarming. The package colony or nucleus needs a second hive body as soon as most of the foundation has been drawn into comb and bees cover eight or nine frames in the hive. It has been estimated that a 10-frame hive body provides room for about 15,000 adult bees. If this is correct, the growing colony needs at least two hive bodies, and a full-sized colony containing about 60,000 bees needs four hive bodies just for housing the bees.

Spring Management of Overwintered Colonies

There are some special points to consider in management of overwintered colonies. An important one is the late winter–early spring check on honey reserves. This period is a crucial one for the bees because they are rearing brood and must increase honey consumption greatly to keep the brood nest warm and to feed the developing bees. Most losses from starvation take place during this period — not during the middle of winter. The first check of the year should determine two things — whether the colony has enough honey and whether the honey is located on both sides of the cluster. The timing of the examination depends on local conditions and the weather. In central Illinois, the examination can usually be made by mid-February, during a warming period when the temperature reaches the 40's or 50's (5° to 15°C.) on a sunny day. If necessary, the check can be made at much lower temperatures; the chance to save the life of a colony outweighs any minor damage resulting from the observations. Even in a colder climate you would be wise to check the bees not later than March 1.

Put on your protective clothing and open each hive briefly to see if it has sealed honey near the cluster. You should be able to see such sealed honey after removing the cover but without removing any frames. Use smoke lightly but judiciously as needed. If there is honey on both sides of the cluster, no adjustment is necessary and you may close the hive. But if the colony is against one side of the hive or lacking visible food, you should make some changes. Remove a comb with honey from the side of the hive opposite the cluster, pry the frames with the cluster away from the wall of the hive, and insert the honey. Without this adjustment, the cluster of bees may die when it contracts away from food during the next cold period. If the colony needs additional food, you can exchange combs with a well-provisioned hive (Fig. 32) or feed the colony with syrup-filled combs or dry sugar. (See page 103.) After looking at a colony during cold weather, you should put a rock or brick on the lid to hold it in place. The bees will be unable to reseal the lid while it is cold, and it may blow off without additional weight.

There is a natural winter loss of bees despite good management. If you find a dead colony, close the entrance and take it out of the apiary as soon as possible. This prevents robbing, damage to combs, and the spread of any disease that may be present. After being freed of dead bees, the hive and combs can be used to start another colony or for supers. Inspect them first for symptoms of disease before reusing them.

The first thorough colony examination should be made on a day when the temperature reaches about 70°F. (21°C.). Look first for the queen or for brood. The absence of brood in a small colony is normal but a colony covering six or eight combs should have young bees and brood. Look at the brood to see if it is normal, without disease, and with no drones in worker cells. Consider the honey reserves and plan to feed the colony if there are less than several full combs of honey.

As the weather continues to warm up in April and May, it is time to do the important spring manipulation called "reversing" the colony. This job consists of moving the colony's brood nest from the top of the hive to the lowest position next to the bottom board. During the winter the colony works its way upward in the hive until it is just beneath the lid of a two- or three-story hive. By exchanging the positions of the top and bottom hive bodies or by moving frames if the hive bottom is nailed on, you "reverse" the colony and provide a stimulus for further upward expansion of the brood nest. You also slow the swarming urge by this manipulation. When you rearrange the hive, place several empty combs above the brood nest where the queen can quickly fill them with eggs. Put part of the stored honey on either side of the empty combs and leave the rest on the outer edges of the brood nest in the lower brood chamber.

Every colony should be reversed at least once during the spring, usually in April or early May, depending on weather conditions in your section of the Midwest. Several other tasks can be done at the same time. You should clean off the bottom board, which will be littered with dead bees, comb fragments, and other debris. At the same time you can exchange hive bodies, tops, and bottoms that need repair or painting. At the end of winter the combs of the lowest hive body are usually empty of everything except a few cells of pollen. For this reason it is a good time to cull old, damaged combs and frames before they are refilled with brood, honey, and pollen. Combs with large areas of drone cells should also be pulled out. Remove all winter packing materials, if you use them, at this time. If you use chemicals for disease prevention, apply them after reversing the colonies and inspecting the brood for any symptoms of American foulbrood and other bee diseases.

Pollen Feeding

Pollen is essential for rearing young bees and developing strong colonies. Newly emerged adult bees also need pollen to eat. In late winter the colony uses pollen that was stored the previous year. If there is little stored pollen, the colony will not die but its growth will be hindered until fresh pollen is available in the field. Feeding pollen or pollen substitutes in February and March stimulates the bees to build strong colonies early in the season. If you want to make additional colonies by dividing, or need strong bees for fruit pollination, consider feeding a pollen mixture to the bees. However, unless you can use the extra bees, you may only create a swarming problem and a feeding problem for the extra bees that require food until nectar is available in quantity. Pollen mixtures are especially valuable to help colonies develop normally in rural areas where most of the land is cultivated or in other areas where early sources of natural pollen are lacking. Without such help, the colonies may not reach full strength in time for the main nectar flow.

Honey bees have such a strong urge to collect pollen in the spring that they create problems when they visit farm feedlots for bran and ground corn. A dry pollen mixture placed in the apiary in February and March will help to satisfy this need and may keep the bees at home. Once started, the feeding should continue without interruption until natural pollen is available.

SUMMER MANAGEMENT: HONEY PRODUCTION

Nectar and Pollen Plants

One reason for the success and adaptability of the honey bee is its willingness and ability to use the nectar and pollen from thousands of plant species of all types. The intermediate body size and tongue length of honey bees as compared with other bees enable them to utilize many different types of flowers to obtain nectar and pollen. Although their tongues are shorter than those of most bumble bees, they are long enough to reach nectar in flower tubes several millimeters long. Honey bees also visit tiny, open flowers that are too small for larger bees.

In general, honey bees must depend for their nectar and pollen on wild plants, or on cultivated plants grown for food crops, pasture, or other purposes. The yield of nectar is not sufficiently large to justify planting crops only for bees. However, there are many ways in which plantings made for other purposes can benefit bees. Agricultural land diverted from production can be planted to clovers and other legumes useful to bees. Shrubs, trees, and annual plants used for recreation and conservation areas can provide beauty and pleasure for people, seeds and berries for wildlife, and nectar and pollen for honey bees. Roadside plants used to reduce maintenance and to control erosion can also provide forage for bees.

Summer honey production depends in large part on the nectar yields of summer-blooming plants. But if it were not for the nectar and pollen of spring flowers, there would not be the force of bees required later to bring in that honey crop. For this reason, all nectar and pollen plants are considered in this section. In the spring, the food reserves in the hive are usually low and the demand for food to feed the rapidly developing young bees is high. Cool and wet spring weather often limits flight and thereby retards the growth of the colony. It is unusual for colonies to produce surplus honey from early-blooming plants such as tree fruits, berries, dandelion, mustard, and willow. However, if colonies have enough field bees, and the weather is good, they may store surplus honey from these early nectar sources. Such surplus should not be removed because it is used by the colony for food until the main nectar flow later in the year. Bees secrete wax and build combs from foundation well during a spring nectar flow. However, unless you also feed the bees, do not try to put a full super of foundation on a colony in the spring. Two or three frames are usually enough.

Honey bees visit large numbers of plant species at any one time and throughout the foraging season. The system of communication within the colony tends to concentrate the foragers' efforts on those plants that give the greatest quantity of nectar and pollen, and have the highest concentration of sugar in the nectar. A plant that is highly attractive to bees when nectar is scarce may not be visited when other more desirable plants are in bloom. When we speak of nectar and pollen plants, we include all plants visited by bees. Most of them are not of primary importance to bees and are classified as minor sources of pollen and nectar. The major, most important, nectar and pollen plants are the few that grow in abundance, usually within a mile and a half of the colony, and provide a fair return of pollen and nectar per flower head or individual floret. An English study of pollen collection by bees indicated that plants offering fair amounts of pollen must be growing within ¼ mile of the hive to be visited by bees. The greatest amount of pollen was collected from the main nectar sources and from those most abundant near the hive. In general, this is also true in the Midwest.

The primary or major nectar and pollen plants of the Midwest, based on their yield and value to honey bees, are as follows:

Alfalfa — *Medicago sativa*
Dandelion — *Taraxacum officinale*
Soybean — *Glycine max*
Sweetclovers, *Melilotus* species
- White sweetclover — *Melilotus alba*
- Yellow sweetclover — *Melilotus officinalis*

True clovers, *Trifolium* species
- Alsike clover — *Trifolium hybridum*
- Ladino — *Trifolium repens*
- Red clover — *Trifolium pratense*
- White Dutch — *Trifolium repens*

Secondary nectar and pollen plants are as follows:

Aster — *Aster* species
Basswood and related species — *Tilia americana* and other *Tilia* species
Berries, raspberry and others — *Rubus* species
Birdsfoot trefoil — *Lotus corniculatus*
Chicory — *Cichorium intybus*
Corn — *Zea mays* (Pollen only)
Cranberry — *Vaccinium macrocarpon*
Elm — *Ulmus* species (Pollen only)
Goldenrod — *Solidago* species
Lima bean — *Phaseolus lunatus*
Locust, black — *Robinia pseudoacacia*
Locust, common honey — *Gleditsia triacanthos*

(continued)

Maple — *Acer* species
Milkweed — *Asclepias* species
Morning glory — *Convolvulus* and *Ipomoea* species
Mustard — *Brassica* species
Smartweed — *Polygonum* species
Sorghum — *Sorghum* species (Pollen only)
Spanish needles — *Bidens* species
Sumac — *Rhus* species
Sunflower — *Helianthus* species
Tree fruits — apple, apricot, plum, cherry, pear
Tulip poplar — *Liriodendron tulipifera*
Vine crops — cucumber, muskmelon, pumpkin, squash, watermelon
Willow — *Salix* species
Yellow rocket — *Barbarea vulgaris*

Plants in southern areas of the Midwest bloom as much as 3 to 6 weeks before those in northern areas. The dates referred to here are those for central Illinois and must be modified for locations north or south. In mid-March, the first sources of pollen and nectar are the maples, elms, and willows. Early fruit bloom, such as that of apricot, begins in April, and apple trees are usually still in bloom in early May. Mustard and yellow rocket are early sources of nectar and pollen. Dandelion comes early in protected spots but reaches its peak bloom in May.

Primary nectar flows, which produce most of the honey crop, are from white Dutch clover, the sweetclovers, alfalfa, and soybeans, depending on the area. Alfalfa is of greatest importance in the northern and western portions of the Midwest, while the clovers are of importance throughout the entire region. Red clover is a good pollen source but cannot be relied on as a nectar producer because honey bees often are unable to reach the nectar in the long floral tubes. However, bees may collect considerable amounts of nectar from red clover in dry years and from the regrowth after the first crop of hay has been taken. Soybeans are a major nectar source in Illinois, Iowa, and probably most other states of the Midwest with large acreages of beans. In central Illinois, late-blooming, full-season soybean varieties such as Clark, Kent, and Wayne are of most value to the bees. They usually yield nectar after the clovers have finished. Bees obtain large quantities of nectar and pollen from soybeans, which are usually attributed to some other plant. There is good evidence that bees increase the yield of beans of some varieties. Chicory is also an important source of pollen as well as nectar. In other countries it is considered a good nectar source, but in this country it has generally been overlooked as a plant valuable to bees.

Smartweed, spanish needles, goldenrod, and aster are the latest blooming of the more important plants. They may yield nectar in August, September, and even later, depending on the weather and the soil moisture. The acreage of these plants is no longer as large as it used to be, and crops of honey from them are also rarer than in earlier years.

Honey bees also collect two other materials from plants. One of these is called honeydew. It is excess plant sap excreted by aphids and other insects that feed on plants. It is most common on trees such as willow, elm, pine, and oak, but may also occur on alfalfa and other crop plants. The other material is called propolis. It is a plant resin or gum collected from buds and other plant parts of trees such as poplar and ash. The bees pack it onto their hind legs but must have help to remove it in the hive. They also collect and reuse propolis from used beekeeping equipment stored in the open.

When nectar is not available, usually in the fall, bees collect a wide variety of sweet substances. They suck the juices from apples, pears, grapes, and other fruits that have cracked or been opened by other insects or by birds. Bees create problems when they visit sugar syrup at canneries, and root beer and other drinks at drive-in restaurants.

Swarming and Swarm Prevention

Swarming is the natural method of propagation for honey bee colonies. Natural selection has favored the maintenance of the swarming trait because those colonies that did not swarm died without leaving new colonies to carry on. For centuries man has selected bees that produced the best swarms to increase the number of colonies. The use of movable frame hives now enables us to divide colonies at will, and we must try to prevent or control swarming because it weakens the colonies and reduces honey production.

Removing frame of honey from a well-provisioned colony. (Fig. 32)

A swarm consists of the old queen, some drones, and 50 to 90 percent of the worker bees of a colony (Fig. 33). They leave the colony suddenly as a group and cluster temporarily on some object such as a tree branch. Later they disperse and move to a new home selected for them by scout bees. Sometimes several swarms from one hive leave over a period of a week or more, and many of them are accompanied by young, unmated queens. Queen cells are built in preparation for swarming, and the first swarm often leaves about the time the cells are sealed (Fig. 34). Swarming is most common in the late spring and early summer periods.

Many factors contribute to swarming. The most readily apparent one is crowding and lack of room for adult worker bees. In experiments on swarming, a colony put into a small hive swarmed in as short a time as 24 hours. Swarming is also associated with the amount and distribution of the glandular secretions of the queen. When there is a shortage of the secretions, the bees make queen cells in preparation for swarming or supersedure. Queen cells are also built in crowded colonies because of the unequal distribution of queen substances among

Removing a swarm of honey bees. (Fig. 33)

the adult workers. Colonies with queens over a year old are more likely to swarm than those with young queens. The seasonal cycle of colony growth, the weather, and the heredity of the queen are additional factors related to swarming. The colony that becomes big early in the season is more likely to swarm than one that reaches its peak later. Swarming can rarely be prevented entirely but it can be reduced to a reasonable level by good management.

To reduce swarming you must plan ahead to provide your bees with young queens and sufficient hive space at all times. These measures will reduce but not solve the problem. You must also be able to recognize the signs that indicate a colony is making, or will soon make, preparations to swarm. One evident sign is a mass of bees that entirely fills the hive. They may come out of the hive in large numbers when you open it. A badly crowded colony often has bees clustered on the landing board and on the front of the hive near the entrance. During extremely hot weather such "hanging out" is an attempt to cool the hive and may not be related to crowding inside (Fig. 35). Any crowded colony should be given one or more additional hive bodies filled with

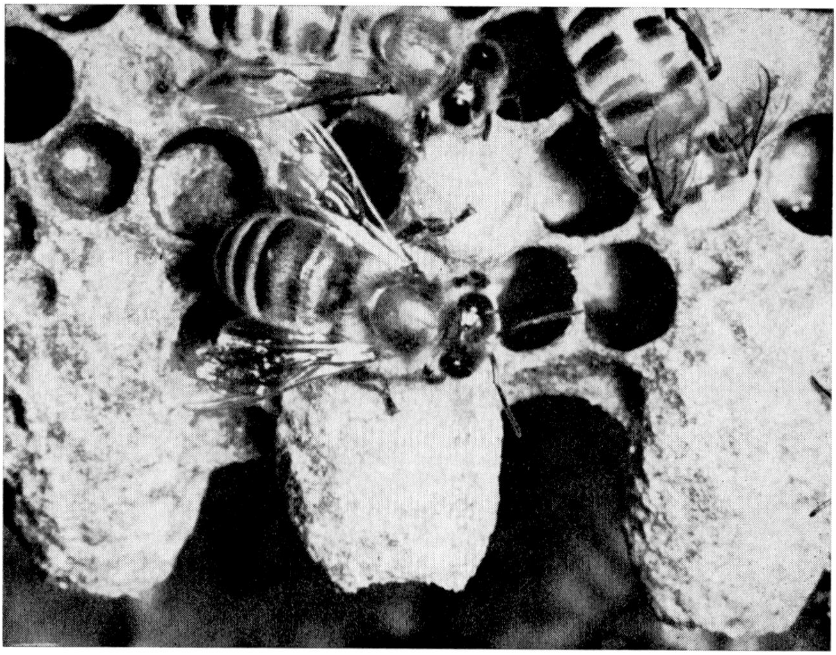

Unsealed queen cells built on the bottom edge of a comb in preparation for swarming. (Fig. 34)

Worker bees "hanging out" and fanning on the front of their hive because of the heat. (Fig. 35)

combs or foundation. The combs will do them the most good; foundation is of little value unless there is a nectar flow or the hive is being fed so that the bees can complete the comb. It is not unusual for a colony to occupy three or more deep bodies before the main nectar flow begins.

Another warning sign of impending swarming is the condition of the queen-cell cups on the combs. They are always present but are usually short and small. The wax of the cups is the same color as the comb on which the cups are built. As soon as a colony begins preparation for swarming, the cell cups are enlarged, their edges are extended and thinned, and new, white wax can be seen on the cups. The queen will lay an egg in the cup shortly after these preparations. When you find these conditions present, you must try to keep the colony from carrying out its plans. An additional super may solve the problem. If not, you can switch the location of the colony with a weaker one so that many of the stronger colony's returning field bees will be lost to it. You can also remove sealed and emerging brood to add to weaker colonies. If nectar is coming into the hive, add one or more frames of foundation in place of the combs removed.

Prompt action is needed when you find large numbers of queen cells in a crowded colony. Check first to see if the queen is present and, if so, find and destroy all queen cells. Additional hive space may prevent a swarm from leaving, but more drastic measures have a better chance of success. For example, you can divide the colony into two smaller colonies or make one or more nucleus colonies from it. These techniques are explained on pages 101 to 102. There is little you can do for a colony after a swarm has left except to make sure that it has empty combs in which the new queen can lay.

Excluders

Excluders are used to confine queens to one part of the hive and to prevent them from laying eggs in honey supers (Fig. 36). Unless they are kept from doing so by an excluder, many queens make a narrow brood nest up the center of the entire hive. Eventually they are forced down as honey is stored in the upper combs, but there may be brood in the supers when the honey crop is removed. Excluders can save time and effort in beekeeping in spite of persistent claims that they are "honey excluders" that reduce yields. It is true that some strains of bees seem reluctant to pass through an excluder but they may need a period of time to adjust to its presence. Put the excluder and first super on the hive ahead of the nectar flow to allow the bees to become accustomed to passing through it. The benefits of excluders outweigh the disadvantages.

Supering for Honey

As the main nectar flow begins, the colony needs additional comb space in which to store the nectar and the honey made from it. If you are beginning in beekeeping with all new equipment, you must add supers containing frames of foundation suitable either for extracting or for making some type of comb honey. On the other hand, if you already have empty, finished combs they should be added to the hives at the start of the main nectar flow. Light-colored combs, not previously used for brood rearing, are best for honey production. Honey taken from such combs is lighter in color and contains less pollen than honey extracted from dark combs. The honey may also have a somewhat better flavor. Plan to reserve your light-colored combs for honey production and keep them free of brood by using excluders or by employing management practices that keep the queen out of the supers.

When brought into the hive, nectar is about 50 to 80 percent water. It therefore takes up much more comb space initially than it does after being evaporated and processed into honey. Colonies provided with supers of drawn comb immediately have space in which to put this large volume of fluid, so they are less liable to store it in the brood nest where it restricts the queen's laying space. Colonies that receive supers of foundation must first build comb before they can store nectar and honey in those supers. The resulting delay can reduce the amount of honey produced and also increase the possibility that the colony will try to swarm. Beekeepers can produce more extracted honey than comb honey because drawn combs can be used each season. To produce comb honey of any kind, they may reuse the frames but must use new foundation each year.

It is important to learn the best time to put on the supers. Some beekeepers do it according to the date, if they know from experience when the main nectar flow usually starts. A few beekeepers put enough supers on at the start of the nectar flow to provide storage for the entire season's crop. Probably the best way to determine when storage space is needed is to look at the combs and shake them to see how much nectar is being brought into the hive. Incoming nectar also stimulates wax production, which is evident as new, white wax on the honey cells and along the top bars of the frames. A change in the weight of a hive is another good indicator of the need for supers. Gains of 1 to 10 pounds per day may be recorded during a nectar flow. A scale colony should be weighed each morning before general flight begins. Otherwise the weight may be affected by the number of bees out in the field and by the unprocessed nectar in the hive. On warm nights the bees process much of the nectar brought in during the day. You can hear the humming sounds of this activity when you walk through an

A queen excluder above the brood nest. (Fig. 36)

apiary at night. The activity of bees at a watering place can give you another clue to the start of the nectar flow. When the flow begins, the bees use dilute nectar in place of water, and very few bees continue to visit the regular source of water. Extremely hot weather, however, may bring them back for water to cool the hive.

There is no formula to use in deciding how many supers to add at one time. This depends on the strength of the colony and the amount of incoming nectar. It is always better to give too much comb space rather than too little, especially at the start of the nectar flow. During the heat of summer, extra supers of drawn combs are of value to the colony by serving as insulation for the top of the hive. This insulation and extra storage space can be as effective as shade for increasing honey production. However, you must be much more conservative in adding supers if you have only foundation to give. Do not put on more than two shallow supers of foundation, or one deep one, at a time, and plan to check the colonies at weekly intervals. Add the first foundation only when you are sure that a good nectar flow has begun.

The first super goes onto the hive above the brood chamber, which is usually made up of two deep hive bodies or three shallow ones. When additional space is needed, you may either "top super" by putting the next super above the one added first, or "bottom super" by putting it between the brood chamber and the supers already on the hive. There are advocates of each system, but experiments have shown that they produce similar yields of honey. However, top supering is the better choice. Bottom supering requires much more work, invites the queen to move into the supers if there is no excluder, and makes further evaluation of the nectar flow difficult. Top supering allows you to look only at the top of the hive to determine when you need to add more supers. There are only two times when you should bottom super. Do it when adding a super of foundation after previously giving a colony drawn combs. However, if you anticipate not having enough completed combs to handle the crop, you should mix three or four frames of foundation alternately with the combs in a super and use it as if it were all drawn combs. Bottom supering may also be of value when most of the combs in the supers are capped.

Initially, an abundance of space is an advantage to the colony and will help it to produce the greatest amount of honey possible. Later, as the flow begins to wane, you should be careful about oversupering the hive. The bees will fill the lower portion of the hive with honey and be better prepared for winter if they have little empty space in the supers.

Removing the Honey Crop

Surplus honey can always be removed from the hive when all the cells are capped with wax. Bulk comb, section, and cut comb honeys must be fully capped for sale or home use. Remove such honey as soon as it is ready so the comb will not become discolored by "travel stain" as the bees walk over it. Combs of honey for extracting can be removed from the hives before they are fully capped. In humid areas, such as Illinois, this requires caution, and combs should be at least three-quarters or more sealed. Otherwise the moisture level in the honey may be high enough to lower its quality and increase the chance it will ferment. Honey may contain as much as 18.6 percent moisture and still qualify for the two top grades of honey. However, honey of lower moisture content is thicker and more desirable. Above 17 percent moisture, unheated honey is increasingly liable to ferment, and at 19 percent it will definitely ferment unless it is stored below 50°F. (10°C.). Even sealed honey may be high in moisture if the weather is humid and unfavorable for evaporation. In drier areas of the Midwest, especially in the western section, bees are better able to remove moisture from the nectar. In these areas combs somewhat less than three-fourths sealed may often be removed from the hives. In any area it is a good idea to shake a few combs to see whether there is thin nectar present, as explained on page 65. Honey removed in the morning will usually have less unprocessed nectar with it than that taken off later in the day.

Fully capped honey, as well as partially sealed combs, may occasionally show signs of fermentation when removed from the hive. Such signs are usually bubbles in the cells and a slightly sour odor. Any such combs should be uncapped and returned to the hives. The bees will reprocess the honey, which can be extracted later, usually without a trace of fermentation. If bees in a particular apiary consistently produce fermented honey, move them to a higher or windier site where they can evaporate moisture from their colonies more easily. This problem is most common in areas having high summer humidity and other local conditions such as evening fog that reduce the evaporative power of the air circulated by the bees in their hives.

Honey stored during the spring is usually left with the bees. Some of it, such as dandelion honey, is not good tasting, and the bees need it for rearing brood. The honey from the main sources, the clovers, soybeans, and alfalfa, is usually mild flavored and light colored, ideal for home use and sale. This crop should be removed from the hives as soon as possible, at least by the middle of August, to prevent it from being mixed with honey of stronger and less desirable flavors such as smartweed, aster, and goldenrod. Leave the partially filled supers and some extra comb space in case a late nectar flow occurs. By a week or so after the end of the summer nectar flow, the moisture level of the honey is usually low enough so that you may remove all the *surplus* honey, sealed or unsealed. Be sure that the colony has 40 to 60 pounds or more of honey remaining in the hive for winter. In the colder, more northerly areas of the Midwest, bees may need 80 or 90 pounds to have the best chance of surviving a long winter. Bees that did not make a crop of honey, or those from which you removed too much honey, must be fed sugar syrup in early fall to provide stored food for winter. Bees winter as well on this food as they do on honey, perhaps even better in some cases.

Bees must be removed from honey combs when the combs are taken out of the hive. This can be done by shaking and brushing, by using bee-escape boards or fume boards with repellent chemicals, or by blowing. For one or two colonies, shaking and brushing is suitable if done quickly to prevent robbing. After smoking the super, give each comb a sharp shake to dislodge the bees into the top of the hive or in front of the entrance. Those bees remaining on the comb can be brushed off with a bee brush (Fig. 37), and the comb placed in a covered empty super.

A bee-escape board consists of an inner cover or similar board the size of the top of the hive, with one or more bee escapes mounted in the center or corners of the board. The bee escape is a small metal passageway with spring closures that allow bees to move through it in one direction only — down into the hive. In use, the board is put beneath the super to be removed with the center hole of the bee escape facing upward. After 24 hours all the bees will have moved down into the lower hive bodies. Before you put the board on, be sure that there are no holes or cracks to let bees in or out of the super. If there are, robber bees may steal the honey. Do not leave the board on during the day in hot weather or the combs may melt. This system of removing honey requires two trips to the apiary and is practical only for a few colonies in a home apiary.

Chemical repellents can be used to drive bees from their filled honey combs before you remove them from the hive. The two materials now approved are benzaldehyde and butyric anhydride, the latter marketed under the name of "Bee-Go." Both are fairly effective in repelling bees and can be used at any time when conditions are suitable for handling colonies. They are applied to the colony on a fume board, 1 to 2 inches deep, that fits on the super in place of the hive lid. The fume board should have a wooden frame covered by ½- or ¾-inch-thick pressed board such as Celotex (Fig. 38). This thick top, white or unpainted, prevents the sun from vaporizing the chemicals too rapidly and thereby stupefying rather than repelling the bees. Smoke the top of the colony well to get the bees moving before putting the fume board on it, and be careful to use the proper dosage of the chemical. Otherwise the materials may not work effectively. Always use caution in handling such products and follow the directions on the label. Butyric anhydride has a strong, unpleasant odor that is repellent to humans as well as to bees. Benzaldehyde smells like bitter almonds.

Bee blowers (Fig. 39) are the newest equipment for removing bees from honey combs. They produce a large volume of rapidly moving air

Brushing bees from a frame of sealed honey. **(Fig. 37)**

In the top illustration, a chemical repellent solution is being applied to a fume board used to drive bees from honey combs. The fume board is being placed on the hive in the bottom illustration. The smoke helps to drive the bees from the frames of honey being removed from the hive. (Fig. 38)

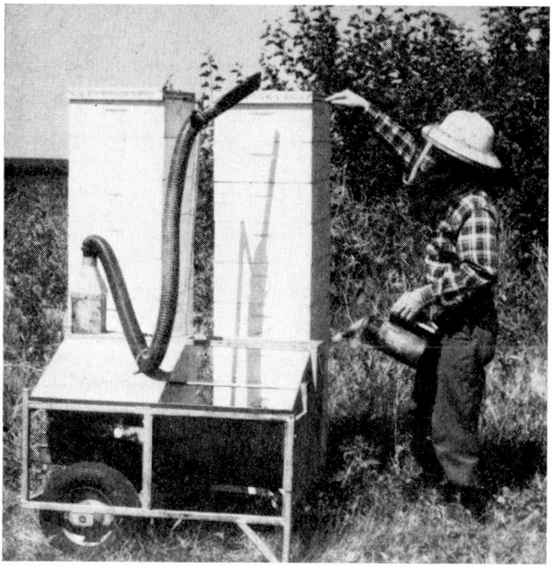

A bee blower positioned in front of the hive. The bees are blown downward toward the hive entrance. (Fig. 39)

that quickly blows the bees out of the combs without injuring them or making them angry. The honey supers are removed from the hive and placed on a stand that is part of the blower. Most models have a chute that directs the bees toward the front of the hive as they leave the super. Blowers are effective regardless of the temperature and the experience of the operator. They may also be used for other routine jobs such as shaking package bees, requeening, and removing extra equipment. The operator of a blower should wear some form of hearing protection. The price of the blowers at present limits their use to commercial beekeeping. However, air compressors and home vacuum cleaners can be used successfully for small numbers of colonies.

Brood diseases of bees are transmitted between colonies in honey and in comb. Combs of honey removed from an infected colony can be the means of spreading disease in an apiary when the extracted combs are returned to several different colonies. For this reason it is good business to inspect for the most serious disease, American foulbrood, while you are removing honey and before you lose the identity of supers from each colony. This can be done by setting the covered supers on a pallet behind the hive while you examine several frames of brood to be sure they are free of disease symptoms. It is usually safe to skip such inspection if you checked carefully for disease in the spring and again when the supers were put on. Do not skip the inspection, however, if any of your bees have had American foulbrood previously or if there is any reason to think they might be infected.

When combs, empty or full of honey, are removed from a hive, they are usually infested with the eggs or small larvae of the wax moth. Such combs must be treated in some manner to kill these larvae, or "wax worms." They will tunnel into the comb making it unsaleable and eventually destroy the entire comb. The infestation comes about when the adult moth lays eggs in cracks and crevices in the hives in the apiary. Adult bees in a normal colony destroy the larvae before they do any damage. For details on how to prevent damage to honey in the comb from the wax moth, see page 108. Honey to be extracted need not be treated but should be extracted as soon as possible. The empty combs must then be treated or returned to the colonies.

Processing the Honey

Honey is a fine food product and should be treated as such from the time it is taken from the hive until it is in the final container. Honey supers should be handled so that they are protected from dust and dirt as soon as they are freed of bees. One way is to place them on clean, washable wooden pallets or drip trays that can also be used to cover each super or stack of supers. Pallets catch dripping honey, keep dirt and bees away from the combs, and allow the use of a two-wheeled hand truck to move the honey in the apiary and honey house.

The honey house, or any room in which honey is handled, should be easily cleaned and not accessible to insects, animals, or other possible contaminants such as dust. The beginning beekeeper usually uses the family kitchen and, except for getting honey on everything, has no real problems in sanitation. However, part-time and professional beekeepers producing honey for sale must conform to public health regulations relating to food-processing industries (Fig. 40). Before building or remodelling any space to use for handling honey for sale, inquire about the requirements you must meet. For convenience, the honey-extracting area should be on ground level so that you can move honey into it by hand truck either from the apiary or from a truck bed that is level with an unloading area or ramp. Plan your extracting layout to provide a step-saving flow of equipment from the apiary, through the extraction process, and into the comb room. Look at several honey houses before building your own.

Stainless steel extracting equipment with washable walls and floor. (Fig. 40)

Removing moisture. In humid areas even fully sealed combs taken from the bees may contain honey whose moisture content is so high that it will not meet the requirements for top-grade honey and may ferment in the comb. The best time to remove some of the excess moisture is while the honey is in the comb, regardless of whether it is to be extracted or sold as comb honey. Avoid storing such honey in cool, damp locations where it may absorb additional moisture. Warm, dry air passed through stacked supers of honey will remove moisture in amounts related to the relative humidity and volume of the circulating air. To handle large numbers of supers, place them in stacks of six to eight, offset from one another so that the air can pass through them on its way out of a warm room. If you have only a few supers, rest them on an air duct and blow warm air up through them. In either case, the air should be no warmer than 95°F. (35°C.). From 1 to 3 percent moisture can be removed in 24 hours. Commercial dehumidifiers can also remove moisture from honey in comb that is stacked within a closed room.

It is difficult to remove moisture after the honey is extracted. However, warm air passed over shallow tanks of warm honey may be of some value. When large volumes of extracted honey are involved, blending the honey with another honey of relatively low moisture content is the only suitable way to handle the problem. In humid areas, such as Illinois, honey removed in the latter part of the season tends to contain more moisture than that taken off earlier.

Comb honey. It is not necessary to process comb honey to enjoy it on your table. Long before honey extractors were invented, man was eating honey in the comb as a simple delicacy or as a sweet with other foods. For example, you can spread thin slices of comb honey, wax and all, on bread or biscuits and eat everything including the wax. Although we probably do not digest the wax, it is a wholesome material often used in pharmaceutical products and can be eaten without hesitation.

Comb honey must be handled carefully to prevent damage to the cappings. After being treated against wax moth, full combs can be readied for sale by scraping the frames to remove propolis and by packaging them in cellophane and cardboard containers. Cut comb honey is cut out of the frames with a thin, sharp knife or with a special heated cutter. The pieces should be allowed to drain in a warm room to remove honey from the open cells on the edges. The pieces can be packaged in foil trays, in cellophane or plastic bags, or in plastic boxes

Cut comb honey in plastic boxes ready for labeling. (Fig. 41)

(Fig. 41). Comb honey can also be stored in air-tight bags or containers in a freezer at 0°F. (−18°C.). At this temperature it retains its quality and does not granulate. Containers, labels, and special equipment of all types are available from beekeeping supply companies.

Extracted honey. There is no neat-and-simple home method of separating the honey and wax to obtain liquid honey from a comb. The most common system is to thoroughly crush the comb containing the honey and then to strain the mixture through a coarse sieve or cloth such as cheesecloth. Heating the mixture carefully in a water-jacketed pan, such as a double boiler, to 100°F. (38°C.) will make it strain more easily. Higher temperatures may give a waxy and less desirable flavor to the honey.

The best method of producing liquid honey requires an extractor to whirl the honey from the uncapped comb by centrifugal force. The job of uncapping is done with a sharp, heated knife to melt and slice off the wax cappings covering the cells on each side of the comb. Power uncappers with vibrating blades, and automatic uncapping machines are available for large beekeeping operations. Commercial beekeepers often remove all the filled comb that projects beyond the edges of the frame. This procedure requires separation of large quantities of honey from the cappings and is not suitable for the beginner, who should remove only a thin layer of cappings and honey. After being uncapped, the comb is placed in an extractor that utilizes centrifugal force to throw the honey out of the cells and onto the side of the extractor. The honey runs to the bottom of the tank where it can be drained.

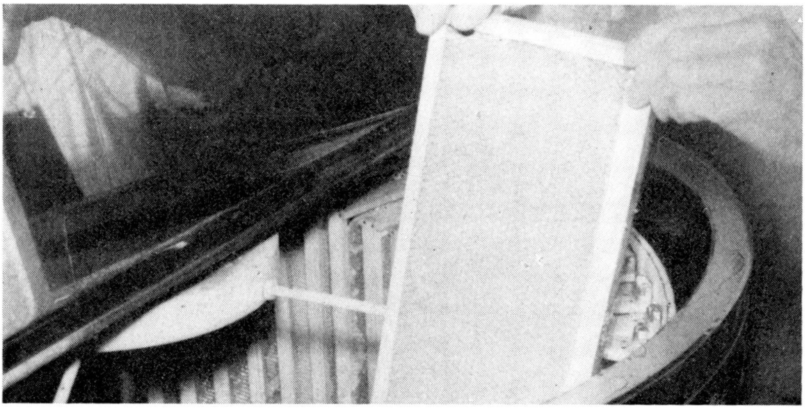

Placing an uncapped comb of honey in a 50-frame radial extractor.
(Fig. 42)

Filling jars with clear, bright extracted honey. (Fig. 43)

Extractors vary in capacity from 2 frames to 72 frames. A 2-frame extractor is suitable for a beekeeper with less than 15 or 20 colonies. With more colonies — up to 100 — a 4-frame extractor is needed, either hand or power driven. The simplest extractors have a gear-driven basket within a tank. Combs are extracted on one side, and then lifted and reversed to complete the job. Reversible extractors have baskets that pivot to extract either side of a comb without lifting it. Extractors that remove honey from one side of the comb at a time, called tangential extractors, operate very rapidly. However, if turned too rapidly, they may break combs because of the weight of the honey. Extraction of honey in a motor-driven reversible extractor is done in three steps. First, about half the honey is removed from one side of the combs before turning or reversing them. Then the second side is completely extracted. Finally, the comb is turned again and the remaining honey is removed.

The large extractors, holding 20 to 72 frames, are called radial extractors (Fig. 42). Combs are arranged in them like spokes in a wheel with the top bar at the rim. The honey flows from both sides of the comb to the walls of the extractor. The natural upward slant of each cell and the centrifugal force make the movement of the honey possible. No reversing is necessary but the extractor must be started slowly and operated for at least 15 minutes to prevent comb damage and remove the honey completely.

The acids of honey react with many metals including steel and zinc used for galvanizing, and may cause damage to processing and storage equipment. For this reason, stainless steel is the most suitable material for such equipment. Piping of stainless steel, glass, or plastic approved for use in food-processing equipment is highly desirable. Galvanized extractors and tanks should be lined with a protective material approved for such use, similar to that used to line honey drums. Many products are available that are used regularly by the beverage and food industries. Most types of paint are not suitable for coating honey equipment and are worse than nothing at all. Some epoxy coatings are also unsuitable because their solvents and other ingredients are not suitable for use in contact with honey.

Extracted honey is most attractive when it is clear and bright (Fig. 43). To produce attractive honey it is important to prevent the incorporation of air bubbles into it. This means that you must prevent the honey from falling or dripping far enough to produce bubbles and foam. Make it flow down the sides of containers or along special V-shaped troughs whenever it is being moved. Use a strainer in such a way that the honey is collected close beneath it rather than being allowed to drip to the bottom of a large container. It is easier to prevent air bubbles than to get them out later.

After the honey is extracted, it will contain some air bubbles and bits of wax. Most of these can be removed by a system of baffles and screens in a honey sump into which the honey flows from the extractor. They will also rise to the top of warm honey in a can or tank. The resulting foam can be skimmed off after one or more days depending on the temperature of the honey and the tank size. It is important to remove the wax before final heating and straining. Otherwise it may change the flavor and appearance of the final product. Honey packers generally prefer honey that has been only warmed and coarsely strained or settled. For final packing, honey is heated to 145°F. (63°C.) for 30 minutes and strained through 90-mesh strainer cloth. The heat liquefies any granules present and thereby retards granulation. It also kills yeasts that can ferment honey, usually after it has granulated. After the jars and cans are filled, they should be allowed to cool before being stacked. Commercial honey processors use flash heating and rapid cooling to further prevent damage to honey by excess heat. Overheated honey is darkened and may even taste burned. Storage temperatures and the length of storage also affect honey quality. Changes in the honey are kept at a reasonable level if it is stored at temperatures of 70° to 75°F. (21° to 24°C.) after processing. Unprocessed honey is best stored below 50°F. (10°C.).

Many beekeepers feel that honey should not be heated. They are then surprised and saddened when their entire stock of honey becomes sour and off-flavored. They may also find that bottled honey begins to leak on the shelf or, in some cases, expands so much that it comes out of the bottle when the cap is removed. All these symptoms are the result of fermentation that takes place in unpasteurized honey of high moisture content (above 17 percent) and in granulated honey. We measure and speak most often of the moisture content of honey, but we are actually thinking of the sugar concentration, which governs the market quality and keeping quality of honey. Sugar-tolerant yeasts are always present in honey, but they are unable to grow in it and to change its composition if the sugar concentration is about 83 percent or higher. When honey granulates, part of the sugar crystallizes out of the solution, leaving the liquid portion much less concentrated and allowing the yeasts to grow and to produce the alcohols and acids that change the honey's flavor. The gas produced often expands the honey out of its container. To prevent such changes, heat the honey as previously explained or store it below 50°F. (10°C.). To retard granulation and to keep all the subtle flavors of freshly extracted honey, store it in a freezer at 0°F. (−18°C.).

Granulated honey. Smoothly granulated honey is a pleasing product that can be handled easily on the table. However, many honeys produce coarse granules, especially after being heated, and are therefore less suitable for table use when granulated. To return any granulated honey to liquid form, heat it in a water bath or in a warm oven to bring it to a temperature no higher than 145°F. (63°C.) long enough to dissolve the crystals. It is easy to make finely granulated honey for home use or for sale. Use about 10 percent finely granulated honey as a starter. The commercial product called creamed honey or honey spread makes a good starter. Blend the starter thoroughly at room temperature with honey previously heated to dissolve crystals and to destroy yeasts. Avoid introducing air bubbles into the mixture. Put it into containers and store it at a temperature as close as possible to 57°F. (13°C.). A home refrigerator is suitable for small batches. A dry, cool cellar may also be suitable. The honey will be ready to use in about 10 to 12 days.

Marketing the Honey

Packaging and labeling. The beginning beekeeper with a few colonies has no problem in disposing of the honey. Often much is given away, and some may be sold to neighbors. As the number of colonies increases and management improves, the beekeeper must decide how to market the honey. Choices include packing it in jars and cans and selling it to consumers, packing it for sale to stores or to wholesalers, or selling it unprocessed, in 60-pound cans or 55-gallon drums, to individuals or companies who pack it for resale (Fig. 44). When the honey is sold, the beekeeper must conform to the requirements of state and federal regulations relating to food and drugs.

Honey sold in interstate commerce must meet the requirements of the federal fair packaging and labeling laws. In states that have similar legislation, such as Illinois, honey sold within the state must also be labeled and packaged to conform with the law. Honey imported into the United States must be labeled to show the country of origin, even if the honey is processed and blended with domestic honey. The following summary contains the principal requirements for labeling honey according to federal and Illinois laws:

1. The word "honey" must appear in bold type, generally parallel to the base of the container.

2. Honey sold by the producer must bear his or her name and address, including postal zip code. Individuals or firms packing or distributing purchased honey must include their name, address (including zip code), and words such as "Distributed by" or "Packed by."

3. Containers holding 1 pound or more but less than 4 pounds must show the weight in both pounds and ounces. For example: Net wt. 16 oz. (1 lb.); Net wt. 32 oz. (2 lb.); or Net wt. 48 oz. (3 lb.).

4. Containers holding less than 1 pound may show weight only in ounces; those holding 4 pounds or more may show weight in pounds only. For example: Net wt. 8 oz.; Net wt. 4 lb.; Net wt. 5 lb.; or Net wt. 10 lb.

5. The net weight must be printed in letters whose size is governed by the area of the principal display side of the container. The area is computed as follows:

Rectangular packages: height × width of the principal display side.

Cylindrical packages: $4/10$ × height × circumference of the package.

Irregularly shaped packages: $4/10$ × total surface area *or* the entire area of the obvious display panel such as the top of the package.

The minimum type sizes that may be used to show the weight are as follows:

Area of display panel in square inches	*Minimum type size*
5 or less	$1/16$ inch
Between 5 and 25	$1/8$ inch
Between 25 and 100	$3/16$ inch
Between 100 and 400	$1/4$ inch

6. Each type size must have an equal clear space above and below it and a clear space to the left and right of the net-weight declaration twice as wide as the letter "N" in the word "Net."

7. The net-weight statement must be on the bottom 30 percent of panels with an area greater than 5 square inches as computed by the methods given above.

Copies of the federal law and additional information pertaining to fair packaging and labeling may be obtained from the Food and Drug Administration, 5600 Fishers Lane, Rockville, Maryland 20857.

Containers for honey should be new and clean. Drums for bulk honey can be reused and should be recoated as needed, but new gaskets are necessary each time the drums are filled. Five-gallon metal cans should not be reused. Plastic five-gallon containers can be reused if they are washed thoroughly with hot water.

Grading. Both comb and extracted honey are sold and purchased by grades established by the United States Department of Agriculture. The standards for grading are not required, but they allow producers and packers to buy and sell a quality product based on grades established jointly by the honey industry and the Department of Agriculture. The quality of extracted honey is measured by its flavor, its freedom from particles or sediment, its clarity, and its moisture content. Comb honey is graded for many characteristics including the number of uncapped cells, attachment to the section or frame, uniform honey and cappings, and freedom from damage. Copies of *Standards for Grades of Comb Honey and Extracted Honey* are available from the Fruit and Vegetable Division, Agricultural Marketing Service, U.S. Department of Agriculture, Washington, D.C. 20250. Some states have additional grading requirements.

Color is not a factor of quality in the grading system but it is important in the sale and purchase of honey, especially in large lots. Honey colors range from water white to dark amber as measured by two systems. In one, the USDA Permanent Glass Color Standards for Extracted Honey, the color of 2-ounce samples of honey is compared with the color of squares of tinted glass. In the other, called the Pfund Color Grader, a wedge-shaped glass trough is filled with honey and matched in color with a colored glass wedge. The matching area on the wedge, measured in millimeters, gives a color rating for the honey sample.

The moisture content and the soluble-solids content of honey can be measured with a refractometer (Fig. 45). Refractometers are expensive but essential items of equipment for anyone dealing in large quantities of

Five-gallon cans of honey stacked for storage. (Fig. 44)

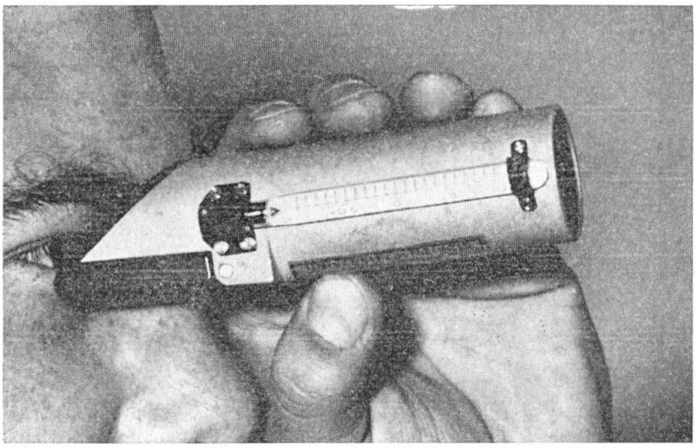

Hand refractometer in use for determining the moisture content of extracted honey. (Fig. 45)

honey. Only a drop of honey is needed to obtain a direct reading of the moisture content. The soluble-solids content, which consists almost entirely of sugars, is derived from the moisture reading. Honey of 17 percent moisture, for example, has 83 percent soluble solids. Honey refractometers have an attached thermometer that is used to correct the readings for temperatures above or below the one for which the instruments are calibrated.

Refractometers and color-grading devices are available from some large beekeeping supply companies as well as from some scientific supply companies that sell instruments.

Beekeepers who have a considerable quantity of honey for sale each

Filling a 60-pound can of honey. The small numbered sample jars can be filled with representative samples of each batch of honey. (Fig. 46)

year should routinely sample each lot of honey as it is extracted or put in containers (Fig. 46). Several samples should be taken from a day's output to get a reasonably accurate representation of the honey. All samples and the cans or drums from which they came must be clearly marked to relate them, and a record should be kept of the number of containers in each lot. A 1- or 2-pound sample will provide enough honey to send small samples to several buyers. If beekeepers send samples and know the color and the moisture content of their honey, they are prepared to bargain for the best possible price for their honey. The U.S. Department of Agriculture provides valuable information about current prices and production in its *Honey Market News*. This publication is available from USDA, Agricultural Marketing Service, Room 2503 South Agriculture Building, Washington, D.C. 20250. The cost is $1 for single copies or $12 per year.

The federal government has operated a price support program for honey for many years. Beekeepers who are unable to sell their honey for more than the support price may apply to sell it to the Commodity Credit Corporation. Such honey is sampled and must meet certain requirements of class, color, floral source, quality, grade, and condition of containers. Information and applications are available from county offices of the Agricultural Stabilization and Conservation Service (ASCS). This program has been changed frequently and may eventually be discontinued. However, it has helped beekeepers and the honey industry by preventing distressed sales of honey at low prices.

FALL AND WINTER MANAGEMENT

The care you give the colony, or colonies, in the fall can be crucial to your success the following year. Because of this, fall management is often considered the starting point in providing strong colonies to produce the next year's honey crop.

Each colony should have enough honey and pollen to last until spring. This means 40 to 60 pounds of honey and as many combs with areas of stored pollen as possible. In areas with long, cold winters, bees may need as much as 90 pounds of honey. A well-filled deep hive body with some empty space in the center combs provides enough stores for a strong colony wintered in two hive bodies. It is more difficult to rate the pollen supply, but colonies with a shortage can be given combs from other colonies or given stored combs that contain pollen. Combs can be filled with trapped pollen as explained on page 106. Colonies without sufficient honey should be given full combs saved for the purpose, or fed enough sugar syrup or diluted honey to make at least 40 pounds of stored food.

Bees winter best on combs that have been used for brood rearing. If possible, do not winter bees on all new honey combs, and be sure that any frames of foundation are replaced with drawn comb. Remove the excluder and all empty supers. If you have no other place to store empty combs, you can leave them on the hive above an inner cover with the center hole open. However, it is better to store combs where they cannot be damaged or blown over by the wind. See page 108 for information on protecting stored combs.

Weak or queenless colonies should be united with stronger colonies that have queens. See page 131 for details on how to unite colonies. Colonies in a single brood chamber do not winter well in the Midwest. If you want to keep the individual small colonies rather than unite them, consider putting the small colony above a double division screen on a large colony. A double screen is a wooden frame holding two layers of wire screen, usually 8-mesh. The screens are sufficiently far apart that bees on either side cannot touch. A rim with an entrance cut in one end lets the division screen serve as a bottom for the top colony while the heat from the colony below helps to keep the smaller colony warm. To use the screen, remove the cover and inner cover of the larger colony and put the division screen in place with the entrance toward the back of the hive (Fig. 47). Put the small colony above the screen after making certain it has a good supply of stored honey of at least five or six full frames.

Good management includes a careful inspection for disease in the fall. If you follow a program of disease prevention with drugs and antibiotics, each colony should be treated after the honey crop has been removed and while the bees are still active. See pages 136 to 137.

As the weather becomes cooler at the end of summer, field mice look for warm places to spend the winter. A nest in the lower corner of a bee hive is just such a place. For this reason it is necessary either to use the ⅜-inch entrance or to restrict any deeper entrance used during the summer. An entrance block, a piece of lath with an entrance slot, or a metal entrance reducer can be used. Do not make the entrance less than 4 inches wide or cover it with hardware cloth because the bees that die during the winter may block the entrance.

The colder the winters, the more the bees benefit from a top entrance to the hive. This entrance permits the escape of some of the moisture produced by the bees. The top entrance also lets the bees get out of the hive more readily during brief spells of sunny and warmer weather during the winter and spring when it is still too cool to allow the bees to move down to the main entrance of the hive.

You can make a top entrance by boring a ¾-inch hole in the top hive body near the front hand hold. Otherwise, you may cut a 3-inch

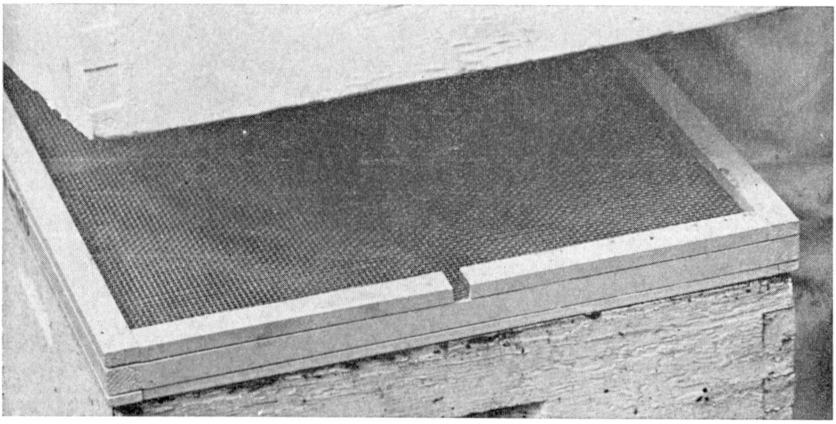

A double division screen in place on top of a hive. The small entrance is suitable for winter but should be enlarged for use at other times of the year. (Fig. 47)

by 3/8-inch slot in the front lower rim of the inner cover. Push the telescoping cover forward to provide access to the opening. Similar entrances can be made in one-piece covers by cutting a slot with a dado blade on a saw. Bees in central Illinois and the lower Midwest can winter well without upper entrances, and you need not worry about their survival if the lower entrance is covered by ice or snow — the bees will not suffocate.

Cellar wintering of bees and wrapping or packing of bees left out of doors were once common in the Midwest and elsewhere. These practices became less common as beekeepers tried to reduce the labor and expense of operating more colonies. They also believed the advice of beekeeping experts who said that strong colonies of bees did not need special protection but only plenty of stored honey and shelter from the wind. In part because the beekeepers took the experts' advice, half or more of the honey bee colonies in many areas of the Midwest died during recent severe winters. At the same time, beekeepers in northern Saskatchewan who had protected their bees with fiberglass insulation and roofing paper suffered only normal losses of 5 to 10 percent.

Colonies protected by wrapping or insulation eat less food during the winter and are better able to move their clusters to new areas of honey within the hive. With the heavy insulation used in northern Canada, the bees cluster loosely or not at all and do not fall victim to "cold starvation" when they lack food because they cannot move to reach it.

An apiary in winter. The snow fence provides wind protection until the evergreens grow taller. The hives face south and the slight slope allows air drainage. (Fig. 48)

Fall and Winter Management

Beekeepers in areas with cold winters should give their colonies some help in surviving the winter. Depending upon the local conditions, such help can vary from wrapping individual hives or groups of four hives with roofing paper to providing insulation or other packing. Wrapped colonies should have an upper entrance and a greatly reduced, or closed, lower entrance. Make sure that the entrances cannot be obstructed if the wrapping moves.

There is growing interest in an improved type of indoor wintering that uses a combination of supplemental heat, ventilation, insulation, and air conditioning to produce ideal wintering conditions. Single-story colonies established in late summer are held in complete darkness at 46-49°F. (8-9°C.) from about November to April. Food consumption is low, and the bees do not rear brood during the confinement period.

More honey bee colonies survive the winter and are stronger in the spring if they are routinely fed the antibiotic Fumidil-B® to control Nosema disease (see page 140). Each colony should be given 2 gallons of sugar syrup (2 parts sugar to 1 part water) containing the antibiotic.

Wind protection is important to good wintering. Shrubs, fences, or other artificial windbreaks help the colonies survive by slowing the loss of heat from the hives (Fig. 48). Snow may completely cover the hives without damaging the bees but the hives should not be located where water may collect. The winter apiary site should also be on a slope or in an area where cold air will flow away from the hives and not collect around them. If your winter apiary location does not permit the sun to shine on the hives or is undesirable in other ways for wintering, plan to move the bees to a better location.

Losses of bees during winter are often high in spite of increasing knowledge about the biology and management of honey bees. Many bees of all ages die in the hive. Losses appear to be greater in very large and very small colonies as compared with those of moderate size. It is not uncommon for more than half of the bees in a colony to die, and for 10 percent or more of the colonies to die. Starvation, either from lack of honey or from inability to reach the honey in extremely cold weather (cold starvation), is the most common cause of winter death of colonies.

MISCELLANEOUS TECHNIQUES IN BEEKEEPING

Caring for Extracting Combs

Good combs for producing extracted honey can be reused for many years. As a result, a given number of colonies can produce more extracted honey than comb honey because they are not held back by the need to make new comb during the nectar flow. After combs are extracted, they still contain some honey and are usually referred to as "wet" combs. Beekeepers do not agree on how such combs should be handled except that they must be fumigated. The combs can be returned to the colonies to be "dried," then taken off, fumigated, and stored. This involves a lot of work, especially when the bees cluster in the supers rather than going back down into the lower hive bodies. Placing the supers above an open inner cover will not always prevent such behavior. It is best to store the combs with the honey on them. The bees move into them quickly when they are placed on hives the following season, and the bees benefit slightly from the extra honey. The bees clean out and liquefy any granulated honey so that such combs will not induce granulation of the new crop any more than will combs freed of honey in the fall. If you prefer to clean the combs, do not do so by exposing them in or near the apiary. This may induce serious robbing that could damage your colonies and spread disease. In addition, the combs may be damaged by the frenzied activity of the bees as they clean them out.

Confining Bees

Bees can be confined to their hives for short periods to move them, to protect them from pesticides, or to keep them from bothering people or animals nearby. Whatever the method or material used to keep them from leaving the hive, action must be taken when the bees are not flying, either during the night or in cool or wet weather. The simplest closure is a V-shaped piece of window screen or hardware cloth pushed into the hive entrance (Fig. 49). Any other openings must also be screened or closed at the same time. This method of closing hives is suitable only

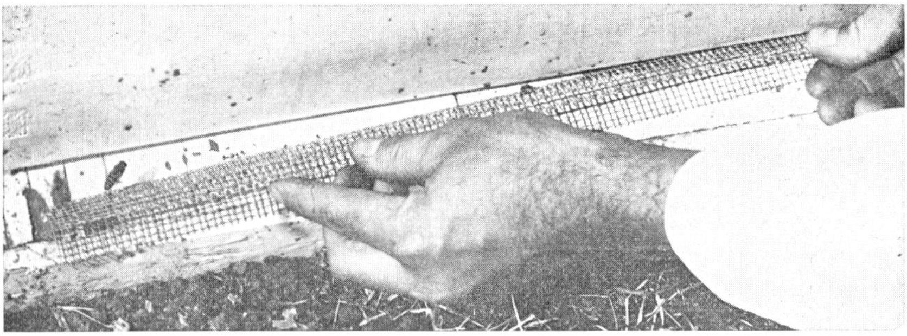

Closing a hive with a V-shaped piece of 8-mesh hardware cloth. (Fig. 49)

A hive with top and entrance screens in place for moving. Bees can move into both screens to cluster and to ventilate the hive. (Fig. 50)

for very short periods when the weather is not hot. With stronger colonies, or during hot weather, or for longer periods, the colony needs extra space in which to cluster. This can be provided by using an entrance screen and a top screen. These screens have wooden frames that give the bees space in which to cluster outside the hive (Fig. 50). A shallow super with one screened surface makes a good top screen that can be stapled or cleated to the hive.

Bees can also be confined by covering the hives with plastic sheeting, burlap, or other materials. The coverings are draped loosely over the hives and held down by soil around the edges. Black plastic sheeting is suitable for only a short period early in the day because it heats up rapidly in the sun. Burlap can be used to keep bees confined for a day or more. In hot weather it can be kept wet to cool the bees beneath it.

Dividing Colonies

Splitting a strong colony of bees into two or more separate units is an important technique in beekeeping. It provides new colonies to replace losses or to increase numbers of colonies. It is also a method of swarm control, and can be used to make up small colonies (nuclei) for rearing or holding queens. To divide a colony you must first find the queen as explained on page 62. If you are unable to find her in a large colony, put a queen excluder between the brood chambers and close the hive. Three or more days later examine the colony again. The queen will be in the brood chamber that has combs with eggs. She is easier to find in a single hive body.

Colonies may be divided initially within the same hive by using a double division screen as described on pages 95 to 96. Place the old queen with about half the combs of brood, mostly unsealed if possible, in the bottom brood chamber. Add an extra hive body with empty combs or combs with some honey if it is needed. Put the double division screen on top of the second body with the entrance facing the rear of the hive. Above it put the second brood chamber containing five or six frames of brood, mostly sealed, and two combs of pollen and honey on each side. This hive body initially should contain about two-thirds of the bees. You must shake many extra bees into it from the combs of the bottom chamber (Fig. 51) because the older field bees will return to the bottom story leaving only the younger bees in the new colony on top. The new division may be too weak to keep the brood warm if an insufficient number of bees is present. A caged queen should be introduced into the top colony within 2 hours for best results but no later than 24 hours after making the division. After the queen is ac-

Shaking bees from a comb into the hive. One or two sharp shakes remove most of the bees with little antagonism if the bees are smoked first. (Fig. 51)

cepted and laying well, the new colony can be put on a bottom board within the same apiary. Fewer bees will be lost, however, if it is moved at night to a new location 2 or more miles away.

Divisions can also be made directly into a complete second hive. In this case, give the new colony more than half the bees and four to six frames of sealed brood. The hive may be placed near the parent colony. However, it is better to screen the entrance of the new hive while making up the colony and then to move it to another location at least 2 miles away to prevent bees from returning to the original colony. Put the screened colony in the shade after you finish the division so that it will not be damaged by overheating. As soon as it is moved to the new location, smoke the entrance and take out the entrance screen.

The same general system of dividing can be used to make small nucleus colonies. For a three-frame nucleus, take one or two frames of brood and bees and a frame of honey from a strong colony. Pick mostly sealed or emerging brood that fills only a third or one-half the frame if possible. Before you put all the combs into the hive, shake two or three additional frames of bees into it. Introduce a queen or a queen cell as soon as possible but not later than 24 hours after making the nucleus. Although the nucleus can be left in the home apiary, it will do better if it is moved to another location.

New colonies of all sizes may be made from brood, bees, and combs from several colonies. Use the same general techniques as explained above and assemble the colony with sufficient bees and stored honey and pollen to get it started. In making divides and nuclei, use small- to medium-sized brood patterns in preference to very large areas of brood. The new colony may not be able to care for a large amount of brood. By using sealed brood, you reduce the number of bees in the parent colony and rapidly increase the number in the new colony.

Feeding Bees

Honey and sugar. More honey bee colonies die from lack of honey than from any other cause. To prevent such losses the beekeeper must know the two periods when the colonies need additional food and the best way to give it to them. The late winter-early spring period, after brood rearing begins, is the most critical period. Feeding may also be needed in the fall if the summer nectar flow was a failure or if too much honey was taken from the hive for home use or for sale.

A comb of honey put into the hive beside the brood nest is the simplest feeder. Combs from hives with a surplus can be given to colonies short of food, so long as American foulbrood disease is not present. Extracted honey can be fed as a syrup by diluting it one-fourth to one-half with warm water; however, do not feed bees any purchased honey. The addition of Terramycin will not make such honey safe for your bees because the drug does not kill the spores of American foulbrood, and these spores can cause infection long after the drug has become inactive.

Feeding excites and stimulates the colonies being fed. This excitement can set off robbing in the apiary, particularly of those colonies receiving the food. To reduce or prevent robbing, and the possible loss of colonies, feed bees late in the day after most flight activity has ceased. Unless the weather is very warm and all colonies are strong, reduce the width of hive entrances with cleats so that colonies can better protect their entrances if robbing takes place.

Table sugar, either beet or cane, can be used in place of honey to feed bees. They will accept sugar in several different forms, including syrup, fondant, and dry granules. Any solid form of sugar must be liquefied by the bees before use and then reduced to the consistency of honey if it is stored. It takes moisture, sometimes body fluids, to liquefy fondant and dry sugar. Bees must also expend energy to remove water from syrup. It is estimated that they use 4 to 5 ounces of sugar to eliminate each extra pound of water in the syrup. If you want to provide the most stored food in relation to the amount of sugar fed, use a concentrated sugar syrup made from 16 pounds of sugar to each gallon of hot water. At this rate, 100 pounds of sugar will make 13 or 14 gallons of syrup. When fed in the fall, this concentrated syrup will provide up to 11 pounds of stores for each 10 pounds of sugar fed. The process is less efficient when bees are rearing brood in the spring. You can make a similar syrup by using two volumes of sugar to one volume of hot water.

Dry, granulated sugar can be used for emergency feeding but is not suitable for colonies that must have food immediately to survive. Place it within the hive in an open container above the frames or on top of an inner cover around the open center hole. Brown sugar, molasses, plain corn syrup, and other similar materials containing sugar should not be used as feed, but high fructose corn syrup may be fed safely.

There are several methods and types of equipment used to feed syrup to honey bee colonies. The beginner often uses an entrance feeder that holds a quart jar. It is easy to use but has some serious disadvantages. For package colonies and other small colonies the syrup in the feeder gets too cold and is too far from the cluster during cool weather. If you use one, put it on the side of the entrance nearest the brood nest and close part of the entrance beside the feeder to reduce the chance of robbing.

The division-board feeder hangs inside the hive in place of a frame (Fig. 52). It holds about 2 quarts and can be refilled without removing it from the hive. It provides food quickly to strong colonies but is not a good choice for slow, stimulative feeding.

The best all-purpose feeder is the friction top can or similar large containers. Five- and ten-pound honey cans, unused paint cans, and gallon glass or plastic jars can be filled with syrup and inverted above the cluster. The feeder can be set within an empty hive body, either directly on the frames or over the hole of an inner cover (Fig. 53). Leave part of the inner cover hole exposed so bees can get out. If the feeder leaks, the bees may collect the syrup and keep it from running outside the hive where it will attract robber bees. For slow feeding and stimulation, punch 5 to 10 holes in the feeder lid with a threepenny nail. For winter or emergency feeding, use 20 to 30 holes. In place of nail holes, you can use 40-mesh metal screening to cover a 2-inch hole in a plastic feeder lid. Heat the screen and press it into the plastic.

There are two emergency methods of feeding colonies quickly. One method requires an open tub or trough to hold sugar syrup and some kind of float on which the bees can land. A temporary cover will give protection from the rain. This is a poor method of feeding: the weaker colonies may not get the food they need to survive, any nearby colonies may take part, and the colonies may rob each other. A better emergency method makes use of combs filled with heavy sugar syrup.

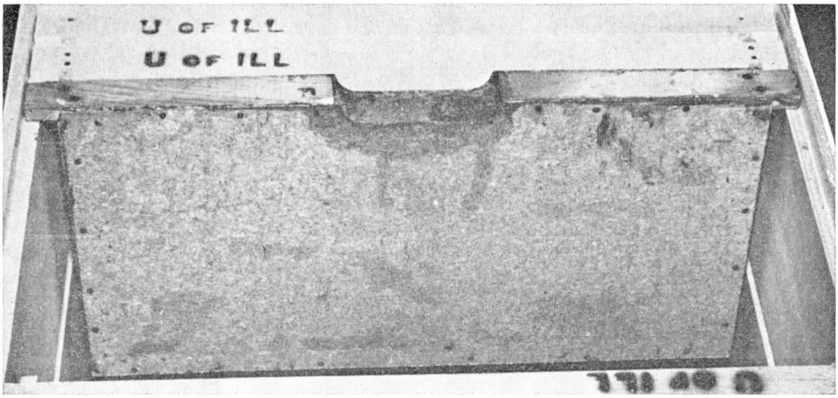

A division-board feeder within a hive body. A wooden float is needed inside the feeder for the bees to stand on when taking syrup. (Fig. 52)

A plastic jar in use as a feeder over an inner cover. An empty hive body and the cover enclose the feeder. (Fig. 53)

To fill them, use a sprinkling can, a coffee can with the bottom full of nail holes, or a garden sprayer free of insecticide residues. Hold the empty combs over a tub or large pan and sprinkle or spray the syrup into the cells of the comb. With both sides filled, a comb will hold several pounds of syrup. Place two or more filled combs next to the cluster of any colony that needs food.

Pollen, pollen supplements, and substitutes. Pollen for feeding bees is obtained by the use of pollen traps that remove fresh pollen pellets from the legs of incoming field bees. (See pages 47 and 129.) For only a few colonies, combs can be filled with the pellets and used immediately or stored for later use. For larger numbers of colonies this method is impractical. To fill a comb, pour fresh pellets from a pollen trap into the cells on one side of an empty comb, tap the comb several times to settle the pellets, and put it into a strong colony overnight. The bees will pack the pollen into place and the process can be repeated the next day for the other side of the comb. The pellets from the trap also may be dried or frozen for later use.

Pollen substitutes are protein materials, used alone or in mixtures, that bees can use temporarily for rearing brood. Among them are several kinds of soy flour, brewers' yeast, casein, and dried milk. When the materials are mixed with natural pollen they are called pollen supplements. Bees eat the supplements much more readily than they do the substitutes because they are attracted by the pollen. Pollen substitutes are available from beekeeping supply companies and from feed companies. You must add your own pollen to make a supplement. Do not use purchased pollen because it may carry bee disease organisms.

These foods can be given to bees as a dry mix in open feeders in the apiary or as a moist cake or patty on top of the frames in the hive directly above the brood nest (Fig. 54). For open feeding, a pan or dish of the mixture can be placed in any open-front box with an overhanging cover to keep out rain and dew (Fig. 55). Large-mesh chicken wire over the opening lets bees in but keeps out other animals.

There are many different formulas for pollen mixtures; they may be purchased ready to use or mixed as follows:

Dry mix:	2 lb. brewers' yeast	
	6 lb. soy flour	
	2 lb. dried, ground pollen pellets, if available	
Pollen cake:	15 lb. soy flour, or soy flour-brewers' yeast mixture	
	5 lb. dried pollen pellets, if available	
	13 lb. water	sugar syrup
	27 lb. sugar	

Pollen cake in the hive above the brood nest. (Fig. 54)

Bees visiting a box containing dry pollen mix. The lid is hinged for ease of refilling the pan containing the mixture. (Fig. 55)

Add enough warm water to the pollen pellets to make a slurry, which you mix with the sugar syrup. Gradually add the mixture to the soy flour, kneading it into a dough. Add extra water or soy flour as needed. Put ½ to ¾ pound of the dough between sheets of waxed paper and flatten to ⅜-inch thickness. If you have no pollen, use 20 pounds of soy flour or a pollen substitute mixture.

Begin feeding the dry mix or pollen cake in February or early March and make it available to the bees continually until natural pollen is available.

Protecting Stored Combs

Honey combs not protected by a strong colony of bees must be treated to prevent damage from the greater wax moth and other moth pests. A beekeeper must assume that any equipment removed from the hives during the bees' active season may be infested. Moth eggs and young larvae are difficult to see. The equipment must be treated to kill all stages of the moth (egg, larva, pupa, and adult). It must also be guarded against later infestation as long as it is in storage.

There are two fumigants approved for killing wax moths: carbon dioxide gas (CO_2), and paradichlorobenzene (PDB).

Carbon dioxide is the only fumigant approved for comb honey. It must be used in a relatively airtight room or container in which you can hold a concentration of 98 percent CO_2 for 4 hours at a temperature of 100°F. (38°C.) and 50 percent relative humidity. Although carbon dioxide is not a toxic gas, it must be used with care as a fumigant. At a concentration far below that needed to kill wax moths it can suffocate and kill humans. Any chamber used for CO_2 fumigation should be designed to include an exhaust system capable of removing the gas in a known period of time. Do not enter the chamber until the system has been operated at least that long. Makeshift methods of fumigation with CO_2 may also be dangerous if the heavier-than-air gas flows out of the container being used to hold the combs.

Carbon dioxide kills all stages of the wax moth and can be used on empty as well as full combs. Unless comb honey is treated to kill wax moths, it may become unfit for sale soon after being harvested if wax moth larvae begin to tunnel it as they grow and look for food. If you have a limited amount of comb honey or access to a large amount of freezer space, you can destroy any wax moth infestation in comb honey by freezing it. Temperatures of 20°F. (−7°C.) will kill all stages in 4½ hours. At 5°F. (−15°C.) only a 2-hour exposure is needed.

Paradichlorobenzene is a white crystalline material that vaporizes slowly in air. The gas is heavier than air, nonflammable, and nonexplosive. Place approximately 6 tablespoonfuls (3 ounces) of the crystals on a paper beneath the cover of a stack of not more than five full-depth supers. The supers should be tightly stacked, with any holes and large cracks covered with tape. PDB kills adult moths and larvae but not the eggs. It also repels moths and should be kept in the stacks at all times for best results. Do not use PDB on combs containing honey because it makes it toxic and inedible. After being treated with PDB, empty combs should be aired for 24 hours or more. After this time, they are ready for use.

In 1981 a new bacterial insecticide called Certan was approved for treatment of empty honey combs. Certan's unique biological formula contains natural bacterium that, when eaten by wax moth larvae, paralyzes and destroys the digestive tract, resulting in the moth's death. Certan does not affect bees, colony activity, or the taste of honey produced on treated combs. It is nontoxic to humans, pets, wild life and beneficial insects. It is a water-dispersible liquid concentrate, thus dangerous fumigant handling and storage is eliminated. Combs are treated by preparing a mixture of one part Certan to nineteen parts water. The mixture is sprayed on the combs with an applicator. Retreatment is necessary after the combs have been reused.

If you have only a few supers of stored combs, you should check them regularly during the warm season for any sign of wax moth and treat with Certan. For larger amounts of comb, it is better to fumigate routinely at about monthly intervals unless each stack is protected by PDB. Without such precautions you may find one or more stacks of valuable combs reduced to worthless webs and debris.

Handling Beeswax

Beeswax is an important byproduct of beekeeping and a valuable ingredient of cosmetics, candles, polishes, and many specialty items. It is also used in the pure form to make comb foundation. The beekeeper has several sources of beeswax including cappings from honey combs, damaged combs, and the bits and pieces of comb scraped from hive bodies and frames. From 10 to 12 pounds of wax from cappings is obtained for each 1,000 pounds of honey, depending on the comb spacing and yield per colony. An additional ½ to ¾ pound per year can be saved from each colony by collecting all the burr combs and scrapings. It is good business to routinely melt very old combs and those with large areas of drone cells, wax-moth damage, and mold. These should be replaced by new frames with foundation to maintain good combs throughout the entire beekeeping operation. A deep super of old combs will yield about 2½ pounds of wax.

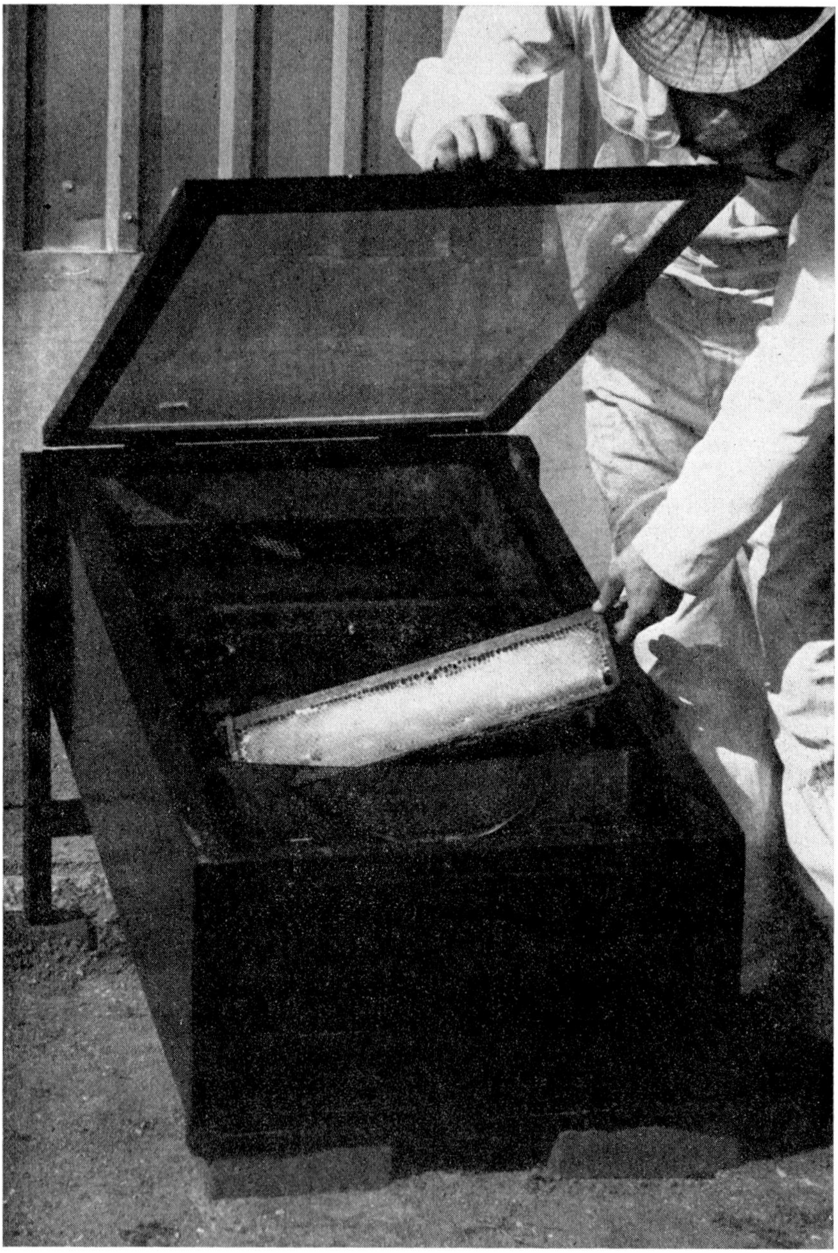

Placing a comb in a solar wax melter. The wax pan is removed through the door in the front. A screen across the front of the pan for the combs holds back the slumgum while allowing melted wax to run into the lower container. See construction details on page 46. (Fig. 56)

Wax from cappings is light colored and of a high quality, and should not be mixed with darker wax. Cappings should be melted with a large volume of water in an aluminum, stainless steel, enameled, tinned, or galvanized container. Do not use copper or uncoated steel containers because they discolor the wax. Allow the wax to cool slowly, scrape any impurities from the bottom of the cake, and store it until you have enough to sell.

Large numbers of combs can be rendered in a steam chest or a hot water wax press. The combs can also be taken to a beekeeping supply company for rendering. There is a charge for the service based on the amount of wax recovered. The material called slumgum, which is the residue left when combs are melted in a solar melter or steam chest, is valuable because it contains up to 30 percent wax. It can be commercially rendered for a fee based on the amount of wax secured from the slumgum.

The solar wax melter is a handy piece of equipment for melting comb, cappings, and other sources of wax. It is a sloping pan within a black, insulated box with a glass top, often of double glass (Fig. 56). The heat of the sun melts wax quickly and it runs into a pan where it can be removed in a cake the next morning. The melter can be made any size to fit the needs of the beekeeper. However, it should be relatively shallow and large enough to expose several frames or excluders at a time. It also can be designed to accept cappings baskets made from expanded metal. You can uncap directly into such baskets, allow them to drain, and place them in the melter to render the wax. A plan for constructing a solar wax melter can be found on page 46.

Handling Queen Bees

The queen is all-important to the colony, and the techniques of handling and introducing queens are important to success in beekeeping. After learning to find the queen and to evaluate her quality, you must learn to handle her and replace her if necessary.

Marking and clipping. The best way to pick up a queen is to grasp both pairs of wings between your thumb and forefinger without pressing her body, especially her abdomen. After getting her up off the comb, hold her against the forefinger of the other hand and trap at least two of her legs with your thumb. Release her wings and you are ready to mark the queen or clip her wings (Fig. 57). Before handling a queen, you can practice the technique on drones.

In general, a laying queen cannot fly because of her distended abdomen, and she does not sting when handled. Mated queens that are not

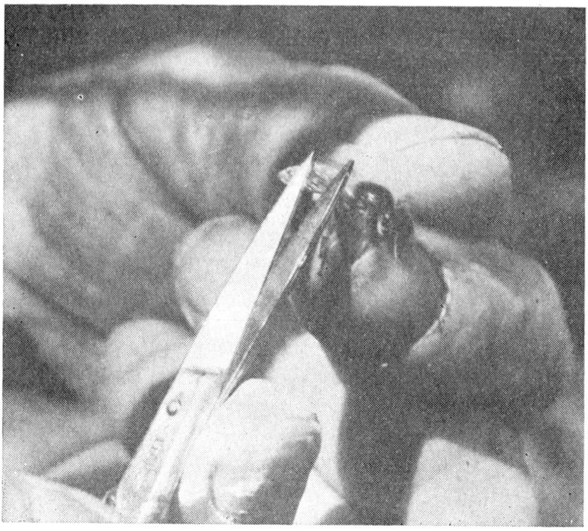

Holding a queen bee in preparation for marking her. Her legs are held gently but firmly between the thumb and forefinger.
(Fig. 57)

laying, such as those purchased for requeening or in a package of bees, can fly readily and will do so when released from their cages. Handle them only in a closed room or within a screened cage from which they cannot escape (Fig. 58), or lightly wet the queen with sugar syrup before opening her cage. Clipped queens cannot fly. Virgin queens fly readily and may also sting occasionally when handled.

Queens are marked to make them easier to find in the hive and to indicate their ages. Queens of the dark-colored races (Caucasian and Carniolan) should always be marked because they are more difficult to find than Italian queens. Fast-drying enamel paint and hot-fuel-proof model airplane dope are satisfactory, inexpensive marking materials that come in a wide range of bright colors. Apply a dot of the material to the queen's thorax, being careful not to get it on her antennae, wings, or membranes. You can practice on drones before attempting to mark a queen. Use a fine brush or, better, a round-headed pin stuck in a cork. Hold the queen briefly after marking her to let the mark dry, and then release her on a comb. In Europe an international marking system of five colors is used to relate the queen's age to her marking. The colors and years represented are as follows: 1984 — green; 1985 — blue; 1986 — white; 1987 — yellow; 1988 — red; 1989 on — repeat sequence of colors. A German bee-supply company, listed in the section on equipment dealers, sells queen-marking sets with numbered plastic disks in the five different colors. They are of value if you wish to identify each

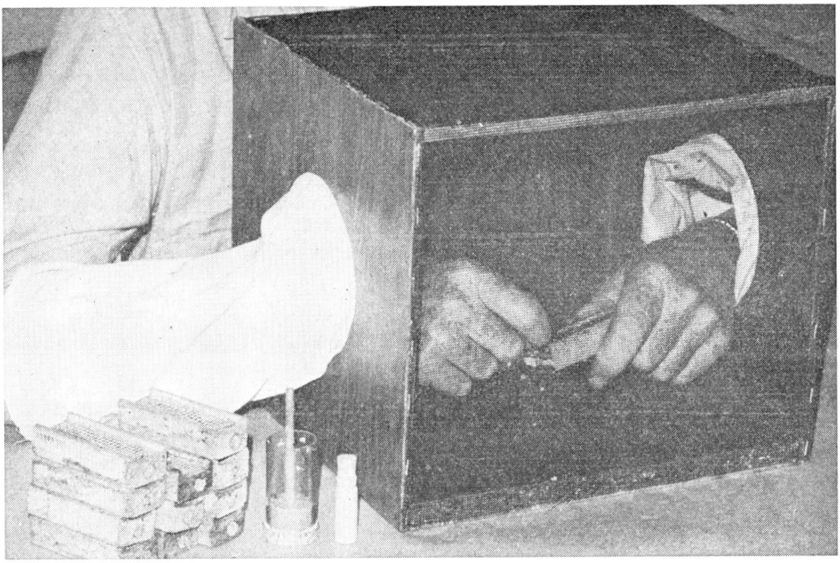

Using a screened cage to confine a queen and her attendants while handling them. (Fig. 58)

queen individually. The company also sells marking tubes that can be used to hold worker bees for marking. (See Figure 59 for examples.)

Queens are clipped by cutting across one pair of wings to remove about one-third of the longer wing. A fine pair of scissors such as manicure scissors can be used. Clipping was once considered to be a method of swarm control because the first swarm will come back when the queen is unable to fly. It is actually of no help because the beekeeper usually does not see the swarm leave and return. Shortly thereafter it will leave for good with a virgin queen. Clipping may prevent the escape of a queen being handled during introduction, but it is more often used as a way to indicate the queen's age. To use it for this purpose, clip the left wing in odd years, the right wing in even years. Clipping may lead to premature supersedure of the queen, particularly if the wings are cut so short that the queen's balance is affected as she moves on the vertical combs.

Introducing. Queen introduction is an important part of bee management. A new queen introduced into a mean colony can change its temper in a few weeks and a young queen can more than pay for herself by the increased honey production of her colony. Poor queens should be replaced whenever they are found, and most colonies should be requeened at least every 2 years.

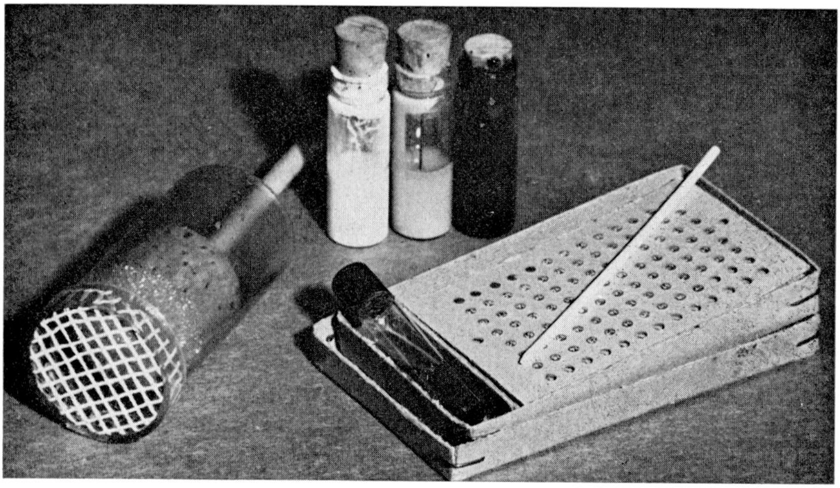

Bee-marking equipment. Marking disks, in five colors, are used on queens or workers. Worker bees held in the tube are marked through the netting. Model airplane dope in the vials is applied with the head of a pin stuck in the cork. (Fig. 59)

The first step in replacing a queen is to obtain a young, mated queen from a bee breeder. The queen, together with 6 to 12 attendant bees and a supply of queen-cage candy for food, will arrive in a small wooden cage with a screen top (Fig. 60). Give the bees a few drops of water on the screen as soon as the cage arrives. If you cannot introduce the queen that day, give the bees water twice a day and keep them in a warm place out of the sun. There are holes in each end of the cage that are covered with cork, cardboard, or a piece of metal. In preparation for introducing the queen, remove the cover from the hole on the candy end to expose the candy.

The next step in introduction is to make certain that the colony that is to receive the queen is queenless and without queen cells. Remove and kill the old queen, if there is one, and crush any queen cells with a hive tool to kill the larvae in them. Within 2 hours, place the new, caged queen in the hive. Before that, however, the attendant bees (workers) in the queen cage should be removed. Many queens are introduced with the attendants present but, because the colony may be antagonistic towards them, the queen will have a better chance of introduction by herself. Remove the cork and let the bees and queen out on a window of a room in which the lights have been turned off. They will buzz and fan their wings but will rarely sting. As soon as they are all out, pick up the queen and put her, head first, into the hole in the cage. If you don't want to pick her up, hold the cage close to the queen and "herd" her into it with your fingers. She is then ready to be introduced to the colony just prepared. Wedge the cage, candy end up, between the top bars of two frames in the center of the brood nest (Fig. 61). Close the hive and do not disturb it for at least a week.

There are several other types of queen-introducing cages (Fig. 62). One of the most useful is the push-in cage shaped like an open-sided box, made of either metal or cardboard. Both kinds work on the same principle, but the metal cage requires the addition of queen-cage candy. Shake the bees off a comb of emerging brood from a colony ready for a new queen. Place the queen beneath the cage on an area with a few cells of honey and emerging bees. Press the cage at least 1/8 inch into the comb. Replace the comb in the brood nest and leave the hive alone for at least a week. The queen will be released when the bees eat the queen-cage candy in the tube or tear the cardboard cage to pieces.

You can improve your chances of success in introducing a queen if you take into consideration the conditions that favor acceptance. Queens are most readily accepted by small colonies and during a nectar flow.

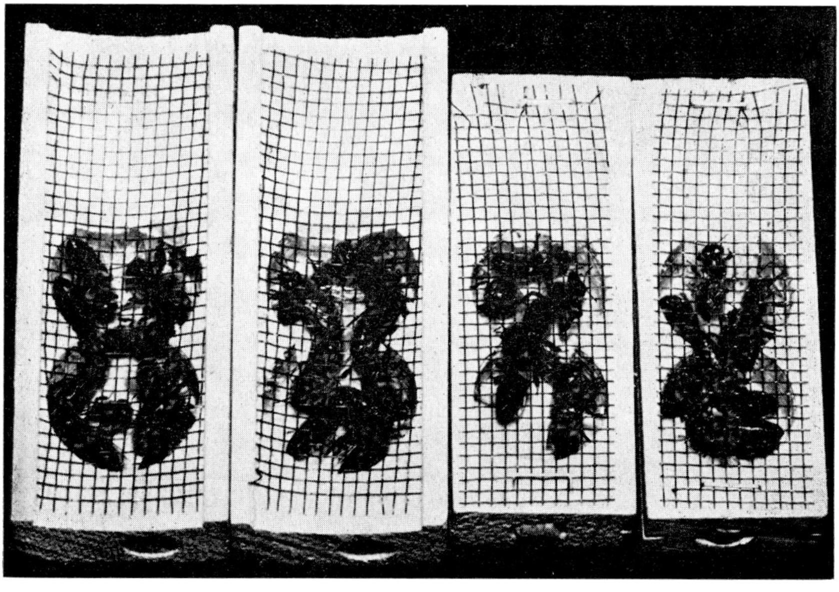

Queens and attendants in two types of queen cages. One compartment is filled with candy that serves as food for the bees when they are shipped by mail. (Fig. 60)

Introducing a caged queen between the combs of a queenless colony. (Fig. 61)

For this reason, you will have the best results by introducing the new queen first to a nucleus or small colony and by feeding the colony a light syrup for several days before and after introducing the queen if there is no nectar available to the colony. If you do not have a small, queenless colony, prepare one following the directions in the section on dividing colonies, page 101. Then introduce the queen to this colony as just explained. When she is laying well, unite her colony with the larger one that needs requeening, after first being sure that it is queenless and without queen cells. You may unite it by the paper method or by just setting the nucleus in the colony brood chamber after removing an equal number of frames. If you have a large colony that needs a queen immediately, you have no choice but to introduce her directly into that colony. Use the system outlined above for colonies being requeened routinely, when timing is not so critical.

If all conditions are favorable for queen acceptance, old and new queens sometimes can be exchanged directly without the use of queen cages. But this is a risky procedure except under ideal conditions and, therefore, rarely attempted by careful beekeepers. The chance of getting a queen accepted is best if she is held in a cage within the colony long enough to acquire the colony odor and to be fed through the screen by the workers. You can improve the chances of acceptance by replacing

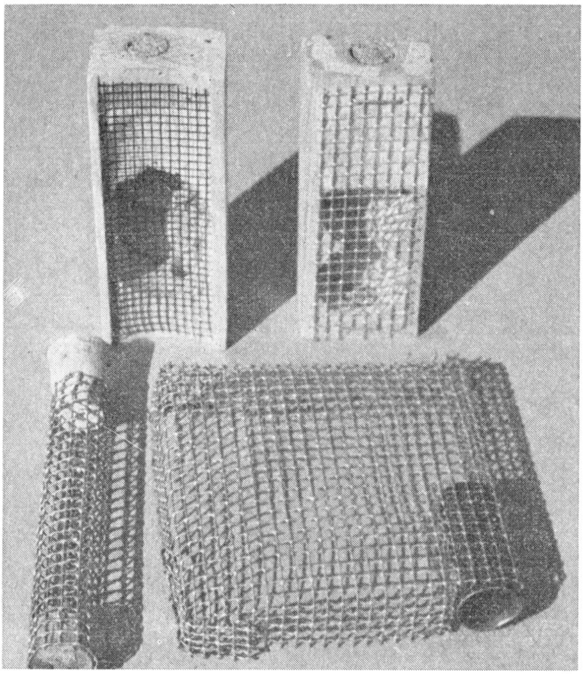

Different types of queen-introducing cages. The two at the top are commercial, dual-purpose introducing and shipping cages. The bottom two are homemade introducing cages.
(Fig. 62)

Extra queens stored over the super. (Fig. 63)

the original screen on the queen cage with 8-mesh hardware cloth when you remove the attendant workers. This larger mesh allows the bees to feed the queen properly, a job that is difficult or impossible through the small mesh of the screen provided on commercial queen cages. Your percentage of queen acceptance will also be improved if you leave the candy hole of the cage covered for two or three days before removing the cover or cork on a second visit to the colony. Obviously, if you are requeening large numbers of colonies, or if they are located too far away for repeated visits, this procedure is not practical. In such cases, be sure that there is plenty of candy in the cages and *do not* punch a hole through the candy to hasten the queen's release. She is much more liable to be killed if released too soon than if she comes out after a delay.

You can make your own queen cage candy to use for introducing queens. Stir powdered sugar into a small quantity of good-quality honey that you know came from disease-free colonies. You will need about three volumes of sugar to one of honey. When the mixture becomes too thick to stir, knead additional powdered sugar into it with your hands. Form it into a firm ball and let it sit for several hours or overnight. If the ball slumps and becomes softer, add more powdered sugar, then store the finished candy in a sealed plastic bag or other airtight container. Because honey is a possible source of disease, it may not be used in queen cage candy except for home use. Candy for queens sold locally or shipped must be made with commercial invert sugar, such as Nulomoline or "queen cage syrup," in place of honey. This invert syrup is mixed with powdered sugar in the same way as described above.

Storing queens. Queens are stored regularly by queen breeders, who must have large numbers available for sale during a short period of time. Beekeepers may also need to store queens when weather is unfavorable for working with bees and when they receive more queens than they can introduce at one time.

The simplest storage method for holding queens as long as one to two weeks is to leave them in their shipping cages together with the attendant workers. When the queens are received, the cages should be separated and placed, screen side up, in a warm place, preferably 85° to 93°F. (29° to 34°C.). However, the cages may be held at a somewhat lower temperature if necessary. Do not store the cages where they receive direct sunlight. Place a drop or two of water on the screen of each cage every day, but be careful that it does not drip onto the candy within the cage. Cover the cages with a sheet of cardboard except when giving water to the bees.

For longer periods of storage, or when you have no warm place in which to keep them, queens can be held within a honey bee colony. Remove all attendant bees from the cages leaving only the queens. If there is candy in the cage, be sure that the hole on that end of the cage is closed by a cork or by some other material the bees cannot remove easily. The queens can be placed in a colony with a queen as long as she is beneath an excluder. Place the queen cages, screen side down, over the center frames of the first super above the excluder. Make sure that the bees have access to the screened area where the queen is located in each cage (Fig. 63). Naturally the colony must be strong enough so that all hive bodies are well filled with worker bees. Put a cloth over the cages to hold in the heat and add an empty super before putting on the lid. Larger numbers of queen cages should be placed in a frame modified to hold them within the colony above the excluder. Put a frame of unsealed brood next to the screened sides of the cages.

In strong, queenless colonies, queens may be stored in the center of the brood nest in a frame next to one containing unsealed brood. The colony must be given additional, sealed and unsealed brood if the queens are to be stored in it for more than a week. Do not allow the colony to raise a queen of its own until the stored queens are removed. In well-maintained, queenless colonies, stored queens can be kept in good condition for periods of one to two months if necessary. It is better, however, to put them into nucleus colonies of their own for such extended periods. They are available at any time to replace lost or failing queens in large colonies. Unless there is a good nectar flow when queens are being stored in a colony, you should feed the colony with sugar syrup.

Queen rearing. Queen rearing is one of the most fascinating parts of beekeeping but is beyond the scope of this circular. When you have mastered keeping bees for honey production, try queen rearing. Books on the subject are available at libraries and from beekeeping supply companies.

Hiving Swarms

Swarms are a problem to the beekeeper and to people who are confronted with them in their yards or some other location. The beginning beekeeper can use them to gain additional colonies or to strengthen established ones. However, the time and expense of obtaining them is often more than the small value of the bees themselves. Experienced beekeepers should consider swarm catching a service and charge accordingly for their time and expenses. In some states a license is needed to perform this service.

Swarms are not always gentle and you should wear a veil and use a smoker while working with them. Prepare a single-story hive with nine combs, either empty or partially filled with honey. Foundation is less suitable but can be used if you have no empty combs available. If the swarm is close to the ground, or clustered on a branch that can be cut off, smoke the bees and shake them into the open hive or in front of it. In some cases you may have to shake the bees into a pan, burlap bag, or other container in order to carry them to a hive. If you are successful in getting the queen with the rest of the swarm, the bees will enter the hive and make themselves at home. They should be moved that night to a permanent location. The swarm colony can be allowed to develop, or can be used to strengthen another colony. If you know from which colony a swarm came, you may put it back after correcting the conditions that caused swarming to develop.

Swarms sometimes come from colonies infected with American foulbrood disease. The honey carried by the bees can infect the brood of the new colony. This serious threat, although not a common occurrence, can be reduced by hiving all swarms on foundation and immediately feeding them 1 gallon of sugar syrup containing Terramycin (see page 137 for dosage). Swarms hived on comb can also be fed in the same way, but the protection from disease is less certain. Whether or not you feed the medicated syrup, carefully inspect the colony for disease at least twice before adding another hive body with combs or foundation.

Identifying Apiaries and Equipment

Hives and apiaries located away from the beekeeper's home should be marked to show ownership. Such identification helps to prevent vandalism and theft because it indicates that someone owns the bees. Otherwise people frequently believe that bees have been abandoned because they do not see anyone visit the apiary. Identification is also essential if beekeepers are to be notified of pesticide applications or other farm operations affecting their colonies.

One form of identification is the owner's name and address stencilled in large letters on the hives or on a prominent sign beside the apiary. The letters should be at least 1 inch high so that a person who is afraid of the bees can read the sign at a distance.

Frames and other wooden hive parts can be identified by names or symbols stencilled, stamped, or branded on the wood (Fig. 64).

A branding iron and propane torch used to identify frames and other wooden equipment. (Fig. 64)

Keeping Records

Beekeeping records are of two general types — management and financial. Management records include all the details of the work and observations related to keeping bees. If the information is recorded regularly, it will soon be valuable for planning work, for increasing your knowledge of the biology of honey bees, and for relating management to expenses and income. Even a simple diary kept up to date can be a worthwhile and enjoyable part of keeping bees. Some of the things to record are local weather data, dates on which nectar and pollen plants bloom, colony losses, colony weight records, and the dates of doing such jobs as spring inspection, supering, removing honey, and extracting.

Financial records are essential for anyone who keeps enough colonies to sell honey. They should be detailed enough to make a financial summary each year for your own information and for computing income taxes and other reports required for business. Farm record books are available from extension service publication offices. Although they are designed for general farming, they can be modified for keeping detailed records of a beekeeping business. Apiary record booklets are also available from several sources in the Midwest. Check with your extension beekeeping specialist or entomologist for details.

Bank-operated recordkeeping services can be adapted for beekeeping enterprises as well as for farm businesses. They simplify recordkeeping for tax purposes and may prove helpful in making short- or long-term loans. Lending institutions need net worth statements and cash flow records in support of loan applications.

Killing Bees

Honey bee colonies are commonly killed when they become infected with American foulbrood disease, when they are living in the walls of a building or in some other unsuitable location, and when they are not going to be allowed to live over the winter. Other management practices also may require that bees be killed.

The insecticide resmethrin is approved for killing diseased colonies of bees whose frames and combs will be destroyed. The insecticide cannot be applied to combs to be reused because treated combs may remain toxic for 7 months or more. Aerosol dispensers containing resmethrin are available from some beekeeping supply companies. Kill the bees when they are not flying, either in the evening or early morning. Close the entrance to confine the bees — the resmethrin causes frenzied activity among the bees when it is applied.

At present, there is no material approved for killing bees as a routine management practice. Cyanide dust and the fumes from burning sulfur have previously been used for this purpose. Because of its extreme toxicity, cyanide is generally not available. The sulfur dioxide gas from burning sulfur is also toxic to humans and does not kill bees as rapidly as does cyanide.

Colonies in buildings should be killed only with an insecticide such as carbaryl, diazinon, malathion, or resmethrin. Fumigants are too dangerous for this purpose. It is important to first locate the brood nest in the wall to learn whether it can be reached by insecticide sprayed or dusted into the flight hole. Sometimes the brood nest is a long distance from the entrance. By tapping and listening you can locate the main group of bees on a cold day or at night when the bees are not flying. Apply dust or spray at the entrance or through a hole drilled close to the brood nest. Use the material at the concentration recommended on the label for the control of bees and wasps. After the bees have been killed, the dead bees and comb should be removed from the wall and burned or buried. The location will be attractive to other swarms because of the odors present. Filling the cavity with insulation or some other nonflammable material will prevent bees from nesting in the same location again.

Moving Bees

Midwest beekeeping is gradually becoming more migratory as more colonies are moved to sources of nectar and are used for pollination. Even those beekeepers who don't regularly move their hives must sometimes move them short or long distances.

The field bees from hives moved short distances — a few feet to as much as a mile or more — tend to return to the original hive location. As they fly out into familiar territory they use the landmarks and flight paths that bring them back to the old hive location. If one hive of a group is moved a short distance, its returning field bees will join hives beside the old location. It is better, if possible, to move all the hives together, a few yards at a time, when relocating them a short distance. Move the bees in the evening or early morning after thoroughly smoking the entrance and any other openings. You may leave the entrance open or screen it closed with a folded piece of window screen or 8-mesh hardware cloth. (See Figure 49.) Careful handling usually makes it unnecessary to fasten the hive parts together to move colonies within an apiary or close to it. However, if you want to fasten them together, do so at least 4 hours before moving the bees.

Most bee moving involves distances great enough to put the field bees into territory unfamiliar to them. No exact minimum distance can be given because it varies with each area and with the foraging distances of the field bees. In some areas a 1-mile move is sufficient, but a good average distance is 2 miles. Naturally, the farther you move the bees the less likely is the chance that some foragers will return to the old location.

The best time to move colonies is about dusk when most of the bees are no longer flying. Early morning is less suitable because the increasing light intensity and rising temperature make the bees eager to leave the hive. If you have difficulties, it is better to have the extra time available at night. A cool, rainy day is also a good time to move bees at any hour so long as the bees are not flying.

The beginning beekeeper who moves bees by truck or trailer should make preparations to complete the job without accidents. Prepare the colonies a day or more ahead of the move by fastening the hive parts together. Use hive staples, lath, or steel or plastic strapping. If you use staples don't put more than four between any two hive parts. Drive them in so they make an angle of about 45 degrees with the crack where the hive parts meet. Lath cleats are placed on opposite sides of the colony and nailed in place with two or more threepenny or fourpenny nails in each hive part. Be sure to smoke the hive well before you hit it with the hammer. Steel strapping is easy to use and holds the hives tightly but it requires special, fairly expensive equipment. Plastic tapes are equally good and are easier to fasten with simple equipment. In hot weather, especially with strong colonies, moving screens should be used in place of the regular hive cover. Cover an empty shallow super or similar wooden frame with window screen or 8-mesh hardware cloth and place it, screen side up, over the hive (Fig. 65). The bees can cluster in the space and ventilate the colony through the screen. Fasten the hive together with the screen in place. Cut an entrance screen for each hive the exact length of the entrance and about 4 inches wide. Fold it into a loose V that will slip into the entrance and stay in place. Seal or plug all other holes in the hive.

When you are ready to load the hives, put on a veil and light a smoker. Smoke the hive entrance well and wait a minute or two before slipping in the entrance screens. If bees are clustered on the front of the hive you may have to smoke them more than once and wait several minutes before they all go into the hive. Place the hives in a truck or

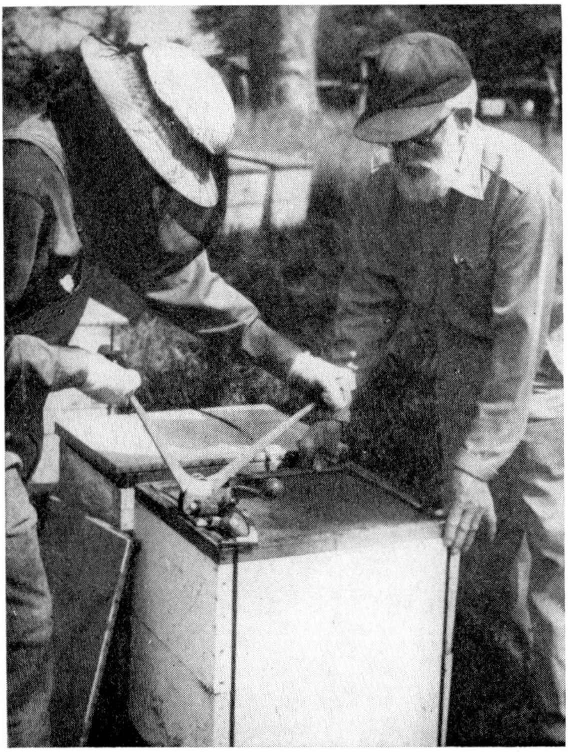

Top ventilating screen in place with hives being strapped. (Fig. 65)

trailer with the entrances facing forward. Arrange the hives as close together as possible in order to reduce bouncing and shifting while en route and tie them in place if possible. At the new location put all the hives in place, smoke the entrances well, and remove the entrance screens immediately. You may remove the top screens at this time or leave them in place with a cover over them until you have time to remove them.

The advanced amateur or the commercial beekeeper usually moves bees without entrance or top screens except on occasions when special precautions are needed. Hives moved regularly should have the bottom boards nailed in place and should be equipped with covers that are the same width as the hive bodies. Proper hive equipment and a flat-bed truck with hooks on which to tie the ropes reduce problems in moving bees (Fig. 66). A typical move by a commercial beekeeper may take place as follows. At dusk the beekeeper drives into the bee yard and prepares to load the hives onto the truck with its headlights off but with the running lights on and engine running. The running lights provide some light to see by, and the vibration of the engine helps to calm the bees after they are loaded onto the truck. With the help of another person, or with a hive loader, the beekeeper quickly places the hives, one to three tiers deep, in rows of five across the truck. Each colony is smoked before it is loaded, and the bees on the truck are smoked periodically if they show signs of unrest. As soon as the load is in place, the beekeeper ties each row using a trucker's hitch and a good-quality, ⅜-inch hemp or polypropylene rope. At the new location, the lights are turned off, the engine is left running, and the smoker is lighted. After the entire load is smoked, the ropes are untied and the hives unloaded. The beekeeper is ready to leave the apiary as soon as the smoker is out and the ropes are coiled.

Hive loaders make bee moving a one-man task. They are also useful for handling honey supers and other equipment. (See Figures 66 and 67.) Heavy-duty loaders can handle two hives on a pallet or one above the other for loading two tiers at a time. A tractor with a fork lift can be used for loading pallets with six or more hives. Such palletized hives are preferred by apple growers for use in hilly orchards where a tractor must move the bees to their locations among the trees. The hives are strapped to the pallets and tied with ropes to the truck.

In most states, colonies must be inspected and a permit must be obtained before bees can be moved into the state. These procedures may also be required for movement between counties. Before moving your bees, inquire about the regulations at your state Department of Agriculture or other responsible agency.

Moving bees with an electric hive loader.
(Fig. 66)

Cradle of hive loader with control buttons. Spring-loaded clamps fit into the hive handholds to support the hive.
(Fig. 67)

Repelling Bees

When robbing gets started in an apiary, it may be necessary to repel robber bees from weak colonies, open hives, and any equipment stacked in the apiary. The first thing to do is reduce the size of entrances of all weak colonies or nuclei. For extended periods, place a cleat over all but an inch or two of the entrance. As a temporary measure, stuff grass, leaves, or similar materials into the entrance so that only a small open area is left to be defended by the bees. To make it easier for the bees to remove the material later, do not push it in too tightly. If you must continue to work, expose as little of the hive as possible. Set supers flat on the inverted cover and put wet cloths over the top of them. Do not set any frames outside the hive or expose honey, syrup, or bits of comb to the robber bees. Under severe robbing conditions cover the open top of the hive with wet cloths, leaving only enough space to examine one comb.

There are no effective repellents available for use on crop plants to reduce insecticide damage to bees. It is also difficult to repel bees from their accustomed watering places such as bird baths and other places where they are not wanted. Solutions containing pine tar, or having the odor of phenol, are slightly repellent to honey bees and may be useful.

Saving Queenless Colonies and Helping Weak Ones

When you are certain that a colony is without a queen, there are several things you can do for it, depending on the type of colony involved and the time of year. The queen lost from a new package colony must be replaced very quickly if the colony is to survive and be productive. Get a queen locally if possible. In some localities, such as the Chicago area, queens are available from bee supply dealers. Unfortunately, by the time you are sure a package colony is queenless, it may be too late to get either another queen or a replacement package. As a last resort in such cases, you may want to put a swarm into your equipment. By giving your name to the police department you can be notified of the location of swarms.

Even small, queenless colonies can usually produce a queen if they have eggs and young larvae or are given a comb containing them from another colony. Insert a comb with a small amount of brood, less than one-fourth of a frame, into the center of the cluster. Queens produced under the adverse conditions in small colonies are rarely very good and should be replaced later, but they can keep a colony alive and growing.

After a honey bee colony has been queenless for about two weeks, worker bees begin to lay eggs. They do not lay in a neat pattern as the queen does. They scatter eggs more randomly and put several eggs in each cell. The eggs are usually on the sides of the cell instead of at the base where they are placed by a queen. The presence of laying workers in a colony makes it difficult to introduce a new, laying queen. The best treatment is to remove the combs in which workers have laid and to replace them with one or more frames of unsealed worker brood with adhering bees. The added brood suppresses egg laying by the workers, and the young bees are more receptive to a new queen than are the older bees that make up a large part of the population of a queenless hive. As soon as you have added the brood and bees, you can introduce a new queen by placing her cage between the added frames. Do not try to get rid of laying workers by moving the hive or by "shaking out" the combs. Such methods are unsuccessful because laying workers can fly as well as their nonlaying sisters.

Colonies in an apiary are often of different strengths, or populations, especially in the spring. Even those with good queens may be slow in gaining size because of a heavy loss of bees during the winter. You can help the smaller colonies by adding frames of sealed or emerging brood and bees from the larger ones. Before making such a transfer, find the queen in the larger colony or make sure she is not on any comb being transferred. Add one or more frames with brood and bees, giving one for each four frames covered by bees in the smaller colony. On a nice, warm day when the bees are flying well, you can use another method to help the small colony. Shake the bees from several frames of brood directly in front of, and close to, the entrance of the weak colony. Select combs from a large colony after locating the queen. The young bees will enter the colony with little or no resistance. The older bees that have previously flown will return to their original colony.

A swarm can also be used to strengthen a weak colony rather than to start a new one. Collect the swarm in a container, such as a cardboard box, from which you can easily dump it. Place an excluder, with an empty deep super above it, over the frames of the weak colony. Smoke both the colony and the swarm and dump the swarm bees into the empty super. Continue to smoke the bees enough so that they move down through the excluder. Find and remove the swarm queen, remove the excluder and super, and replace the hive cover.

These methods of helping weaker colonies do two things for you. They reduce the size of the large colonies and aid in swarm prevention. They also produce colonies of more equal strength that can be manipulated more uniformly. Honey production can be improved by bringing the colonies into a nectar flow neither weak nor so big that they are ready to swarm. Brood added to package colonies will also help them to reach full strength much faster than colonies not given such help.

Transferring Bees

Many publications have been written about transferring bees from primitive hives, buildings, and trees to modern hives. They usually suggest tearing open the colony and fitting the combs into new frames. Another method uses a screen cone or bee escape over the flight hole so that bees can come out but not reenter the hole. The displaced bees are supposed to enter a hive located beside the entrance.

Transferring bees is no job for the beginner, and it is not worthwhile for the experienced who can obtain all the bees they need by dividing their colonies. Rather than risk the possibility of being seriously stung for little reward, you should resist the temptation to transfer a colony and, instead, should kill the bees or leave them alone. If you want to try removing bees from a building, do the job for a fee, not just for the bees and any honey in the colony. You might consider transferring bees as a sport or a form of recreation, but it is not a good way to begin beekeeping or to increase your number of colonies.

Trapping Pollen

Trapped pollen is of value for feeding bees. It will become increasingly important as natural sources of pollen become scarcer and as more colonies are used for spring pollination of crops such as apples. A market has developed for pollen for use by commercial beekeepers to feed their colonies.

Pollen traps vary in some features of design but all of the available models have a double screen of 5-mesh hardware cloth that scrapes some of the pollen pellets from the legs of incoming pollen-collecting bees (Fig. 68). The pollen falls through another screen into a box or tray where it is inaccessible to the colony and can be removed without disturbing the bees. The traps remove only part of the incoming pollen and they stimulate colonies to collect more. They probably reduce honey production if used on the same colony for more than a week or two at a time. However, the value of the pollen for supplemental feeding can easily offset the loss of part of the honey crop from a few colonies.

The pollen should be collected from the traps at least three times per week and dried or frozen for storage. If you wish to dry the pollen, use shallow layers exposed to the air or heated at moderate temperatures, not over 140°F. (60°C.), in an oven. Ants, wax-moth larvae, and small beetles are often found in the pollen. The ants can be discouraged by use of sticky barriers or pans of oil surrounding the supports for the hive (Fig. 68). Rain ruins pollen quickly and all traps seem to be vulnerable to it. In selecting a pollen trap, choose the design that will best keep rain out and provide the maximum area of ventilation for the hive. A plan for building a pollen trap is given on page 48.

Pollen trap and stand that fit beneath the hive. Bees enter through the wide entrance and crawl upward into the hive through the double screen. The pollen falls through the bottom screen and is removed on a tray from the rear of the hive. (Modified from an original design by the Ontario Agricultural College in Canada.) (Fig. 68)

Uniting Bees

Weak colonies are often liabilities instead of assets. This is especially true when they have poor queens or have been queenless so long that laying workers are present. Such colonies will not make any honey and are not good risks for wintering. They should be united with a moderately strong colony with a good queen. Uniting two weak colonies will not produce one strong colony.

Uniting a small colony with a larger one by the paper method. (Fig. 69)

Kill any queen present in the weak colony and place the hive, without a bottom board, above a single sheet of newspaper over the open top of the stronger colony (Fig. 69). Punch a few small slits in the paper to make it easier for the bees to remove it. In hot weather wait until late afternoon so the heat and lack of ventilation will not damage the upper colony. The bees will remove the paper with little fighting and the colonies will be united. Any colonies united in the fall should be checked again before winter to be sure that the clusters are together and that the hive has sufficient stores for winter.

Although the newspaper method is the safest way to unite bees and causes few losses of bees, colonies may be united without the precautions mentioned above. You can unite bees from several hives in the same way as you can make divides and nuclei from frames of brood and bees from several colonies. If none of the queens are of special value, put all the bees together without finding or killing any queens. The youngest queen is most likely to survive and only rarely will all of the queens be killed. The united colony should be checked after a week or two for the presence of the queen and its general condition and arrangement. When colonies are united, the returning field bees from the relocated hives are disoriented briefly. They soon join the united colony and settle down with only minor problems.

DISEASES, PESTS, AND PESTICIDES AFFECTING HONEY BEES

The honey bee is subject to many diseases and pests as are other insects and livestock. The diseases differ in their severity but all of them can be prevented or controlled by proper management. Such management includes knowing and recognizing the symptoms of diseases, inspecting colonies regularly, and applying control measures promptly when disease is found. Drugs and antibiotics are effective in preventing disease but cannot substitute for good management. They must be used at the proper time and dosage to avoid contamination of honey.

The diseases of bees are usually divided into two classes — those that attack the developing stages (the brood), and those that attack adult bees. In general, the brood diseases are more serious and their symptoms are more definite and distinctive than those of the adult diseases. It takes experience and close observation to distinguish a diseased larva or pupa from a healthy one, or one dead from other causes. This experience can be gained only by frequent examination of the combs of a colony. This is one of the reasons why the beginning beekeeper must open the colonies regularly.

Brood Diseases

American foulbrood. This disease, usually called AFB, has always been a problem in beekeeping. It is caused by a bacterium, or germ, called *Bacillus larvae,* which has a long-lived, resistant spore that can remain dormant for more than 50 years in combs and honey. When food containing spores is fed to a young larva, the spores germinate and multiply until they kill the developing bee just after its cell is sealed. Until that time no symptoms of the infection are visible except perhaps a slight graying or dullness of the usually glistening white immature insect. The infected bee dies as a larva stretched lengthwise in the cell, or as a new pupa with the body features of an adult bee. The capping of an infected cell may be slightly sunken and darker than healthy ones around it. Adult bees often puncture the cappings of in-

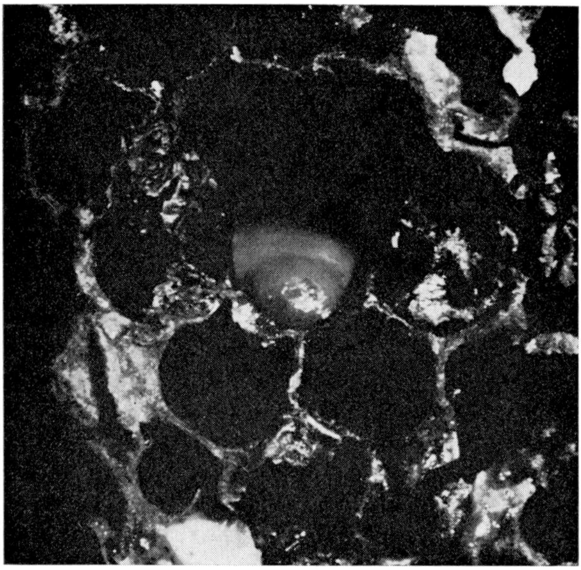

A dead larva infected with American foulbrood shown head on. It shows the typical melted appearance, even color, and straight position in the cell. The cell walls and cappings were broken to expose the larva.
(Fig. 70)

fected cells and may remove them entirely. Since there are also holes in cells containing healthy larvae being capped, you must learn to distinguish them from abnormal ones. Worker, drone, and queen larvae and pupae are all susceptible to American foulbrood.

The larva or pupa that dies of AFB always lies perfectly straight on the lower side of the cell (Fig. 70). It loses its pearly white color and rapidly turns light brown similar to the color of coffee with cream. As it continues to decay and become dried, it turns dark brown and, finally, it turns into a black dried scale on the lower side of the cell. Other characteristic symptoms of American foulbrood are the somewhat glossy, uniform color of the dead larva or pupa, and the melted look as the body and the body wall rot. Sometimes the bacteria make the pupal tongue stick to the top of the cell. When this happens, the tongue looks like a smooth, fine thread extending vertically across the cell. However, many advanced cases of American foulbrood do not show this symptom.

The bacteria rot the skin of the developing bee and turn the body into a slimy mass that becomes stickier as it dries. This condition is the basis for the "ropiness" test that can be used to aid in diagnosing the disease. When making a diagnosis, you should carefully remove the capping from a cell that appears abnormal, but *do not touch its contents* until you have closely examined their color, position, and other features. Only then should you touch the dead remains with a straw, toothpick, or match stick. Do not use a hive tool for this purpose. Watch to see what happens when you poke the remains. The larva or pupa with AFB will often collapse into a rubbery mass. Stir it with the stick and withdraw it slowly. If it strings or "ropes" out, see how far it will pull out. More important however, is what happens when the string breaks. If the cell is infected with American foulbrood, the mass on the stick should look like a drop with no sign of the drawn-out string. The remains left in the cell should be smooth with no sign of the drawn-out piece. In contrast, a cell infected with European foulbrood usually strings out and breaks off like a piece of dough or taffy.

The odor of American foulbrood is distinctive but *is not* a reliable indicator because people's sensitivities to odors vary so widely, and the odor may be strong or weak. The odor is similar to that of old-fashioned animal glues that are now rarely used. However, it is better to rely on your eyes to diagnose the disease.

The black scales resulting from infection with American foulbrood blend with the color of dark combs and are difficult to recognize. To see them, hold the comb so that sunlight strikes the lower side of the cells. The faint outline of the scale and the slightly raised head portion of it will then be evident. When examining combs of dead colonies, look for any sign of scales. They may be the only disease symptom present in the hive.

American foulbrood is spread by the exchange of infected honey and combs between colonies, either by the beekeeper or by robber bees. Infected colonies rarely recover and as they become weakened and die, they are often robbed by bees from nearby colonies. Reduce the size of the entrance of any weak colony, and close any dead colony and remove it from the apiary. You must be certain that weak or dead colonies do not have AFB before you exchange any combs or honey from them or unite them with other colonies.

If you need help in inspecting your colonies or diagnosing disease, it is available in most states on request from the Department of Agriculture. The best time for inspection is the period from mid-March to about June 1st, before the nectar flow begins. Samples of diseased comb for laboratory examination can be sent to the Bioenvironmental Bee Laboratory, USDA-SEA, Building 476, BARC-East, Beltsville, Maryland 20705. Select a sample of brood comb about 5 inches square that contains large numbers of affected cells. Mail it in a strong cardboard or wooden box *without* an airtight wrapping. Samples that are crushed or moldy because of improper packaging make diagnosis impossible.

Disease control is primarily the responsibility of each beekeeper, who must learn the symptoms of the diseases and inspect the colonies carefully for the presence of American foulbrood. At the minimum, inspect your bees in the spring and the fall. It may also pay you to inspect colonies before putting on the honey supers and when you remove honey. At least one of the latter two inspections is essential if you have previously lost any colonies to American foulbrood. Bee diseases are spread more often within beekeeping operations than between them, and lack of inspection is a major cause of such spread.

Most state laws require the burning of colonies of bees infected with American foulbrood. The colony must be killed and all the contents of the hive burned, including bees, combs, frames, and honey. (See page 122 for directions for killing bees.) The fire should be built in a pit and the ashes covered afterwards. The cover, bottom board, and hive bodies should be scraped and then scorched. A blowtorch or weed burner is suitable for scorching small quantities of equipment. For large quantities, brush the inside surfaces with a mixture of one-half gasoline and one-half motor oil and stack the hive bodies four or five high. Light the stacks and allow them to burn long enough to lightly char the wood. Place a cover over the stack to put out the fire. Afterward, separate the hive bodies and be sure that all the fire is out or it may later burn up the equipment.

Many methods of saving and treating diseased colonies have been tried and found to be ineffective. These methods sometimes require more expense and labor than the value of the diseased colonies. When not done properly, the treatments often spread disease. Inspection and prevention are the best methods of control. The only approved medicinal agent for preventive feeding for American foulbrood is oxytetracycline HCl (Terramycin). This material does not kill the disease organism but prevents its growth when present in low concentrations in the food fed by the workers to larvae.

Terramycin is relatively unstable in honey or syrup solutions and is best used as a dust in mixture with powdered sugar. It is available in at least two forms and in three concentrations of the active ingredient. Terramycin TM-50D contains 50 grams active material per pound, Terramycin Animal Formula Soluble Powder (TAFSP), usually called TM-25, contains 25 grams active material per pound, and Terramycin Feed Premix (TM-10) contains 10 grams active material per pound. All of these compounds must be diluted with powdered sugar for application to colonies of bees. A ready-to-feed mixture is also available. The desired dosage of 200 milligrams per ounce feeding can be achieved as follows:

Product formulation	Amount of drug	Amount of sugar
10 g/lb.	2½ tsp. (⅓ oz.)	3 tbsp. (1 oz.)
25 g/lb.	1 tsp. (⅛ oz.)	3 tbsp. (1 oz.)
50 g/lb.	½ tsp. (1/16 oz.)	3 tbsp. (1 oz.)

For larger quantities, increase the amounts according to the number of colonies to be fed, or follow directions supplied by the manufacturer.

Place 3 level tablespoonfuls of the drug-sugar mixture over the top of the frames at the outer edge of the brood nest. Three dustings at 4- to 5-day intervals are recommended. The drug in this concentration is toxic to larvae and should be kept from contact with brood. Decrease the amount of the drug mixture given to weak colonies.

Any medicinal agents or mixtures should be applied only after inspection in the spring and at least 4 weeks before the main nectar flow. They may be used again after the honey is removed in late summer or during the fall. Use them with care at the proper dosages, and follow the directions and precautions on the labels. The products are available at beekeeping supply companies, livestock supply stores, and feed stores.

European foulbrood. This brood disease, usually called EFB, appears to be much less common than American foulbrood in the Midwest. It is caused by a bacterium, *Streptococcus pluton,* that does not always kill the infected larva but sometimes may kill large numbers of larvae very rapidly. The disease and its symptoms are highly variable, probably because of the presence of several other organisms in the dead and dying larvae. EFB does not usually kill the colony, but a heavy infection will seriously reduce honey production. It is not necessary for beekeepers to kill colonies infected with EFB, but it is essential to be able to distinguish European from American foulbrood disease.

Larvae infected with EFB usually die while still coiled in the bottom of the unsealed cell. This is distinctly different from what occurs with AFB. In some instances the disease may also affect sealed larvae and, rarely, pupae. When this happens, the larva usually dies in a partially curled or distorted position, only rarely lying straight on the lower side of the cell as it does when infected with American foulbrood. Affected larvae are not always the same color, as with AFB, but may be yellow, gray, or brown, or a mixture of these colors. The air tubes, or tracheae, often remain visible in the larva infected with EFB. Their presence helps to distinguish the disease from AFB, in which no tracheae can be seen in the decaying brood. The odor of European foulbrood may be described as being sour or similar to the odor of rotting fish. As with AFB, it is best not to use odor for diagnosis because of its variability and the differences in the ability of people to distinguish odors.

The typical consistency of EFB-infected larvae is doughlike. The remains may be somewhat ropy but less slimy and elastic than those of AFB-infected bees. When pulled out of the cell, the material reacts like dough or taffy when the pieces separate. Dried scales in comb may appear similar to those of American foulbrood if lying straight in the cells. However, most of them are turned or twisted in the cell and can be easily removed, whereas the scales of AFB are difficult to remove. Worker, drone, and queen larvae are all susceptible to EFB.

European foulbrood may be controlled by use of Terramycin in the same way as American foulbrood. This dual control exerted by the antibiotic makes it a good choice for preventive feeding where both diseases are a threat. Honey bee strains vary in their resistance to European foulbrood. When only one or a few colonies are affected, they should be requeened with a different strain of bees. The organisms associated with European foulbrood are usually present even in hives that do not show symptoms of disease. The susceptibility of the particular strain of bees and, perhaps, nutritional factors bring about the appearance of the disease at damaging levels.

Sacbrood. Sacbrood disease is caused by a virus and is common but rarely serious in the Midwest. Like European foulbrood, it must be distinguished from American foulbrood.

The presence of sacbrood-infected larvae produces a spotted appearance of the brood combs, a condition shared with all other brood diseases. The larvae die extended on the lower side of the sealed cells, and after they die part or all of the cappings may be removed by the adult bees. The skin of the dead larva does not rot as it does if the larva has died of foulbrood. Instead, it remains tough and encloses the watery contents like a sack, giving the disease its name. The head of the dead larva darkens more rapidly than the rest of the body and stays upright in the cell. It has been compared with the tip of a wooden Dutch shoe (Fig. 71). The elevated head of the completely dried larva remains readily visible in the cell. Such a scale is easily removed from the cell.

Sacbrood is most common in the spring, usually affecting only a few cells in a comb. Occasionally a very susceptible queen may have large

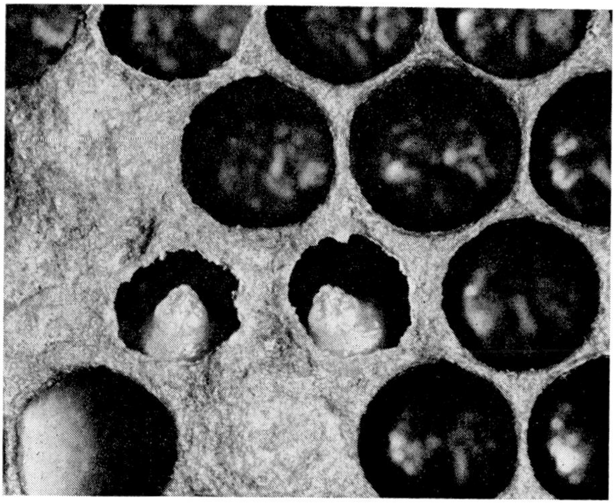

Two larvae, in uncapped cells, infected with sacbrood disease. (Fig. 71)

numbers of affected larvae. The disease usually requires no treatment. In severe cases, the colony should be requeened with a young queen from a different strain of bees.

Other brood diseases. Another brood disease has become established in many areas of the Midwest. It is called chalkbrood and is caused by a fungus organism called *Ascosphaera apis.* The fungus kills the larva after it is stretched out in the cell, turning it into a hard, white mummy. It may be covered with small black spots, which are the reproductive bodies of the fungus. Such mummies can be seen in the combs of infected colonies and on the landing boards of the hives where they are often dropped by house-cleaning bees. The disease may become severe in some colonies but is not expected to be a serious problem for beekeepers. There are probably differences in resistance among strains of bees, and requeening with a different strain may be of value in some cases. No control measures using drugs or chemicals are approved as yet.

Diseases too rare to discuss are parafoulbrood, a bacterial disease similar to European foulbrood, and stonebrood, caused by a fungus. Plant poisoning of brood is also rare in the Midwest.

Chilled or starved brood may sometimes be confused with diseased brood. Such brood is usually found outside the cluster area of small colonies and lacks most of the specific symptoms of the diseases because all brood stages may be affected. When the weather warms or the colony receives a new supply of food, the bees will quickly clean out all of the dead brood.

Adult Bee Diseases

Adult bees suffer from several diseases that are usually found in most colonies but rarely cause serious damage. In some parts of the world, a mite, *Acarapis woodi,* causes acarine disease when it infests the tracheae or breathing tubes of the bees' thorax. The Federal Honey Bee Act, enacted August 31, 1922, was amended in recent years to prevent the introduction and spread of diseases and parasites harmful to honey bees in the United States. This internal parasitic mite, however, was confirmed July 1984 in honey bee colonies in the state of Texas. It is believed that the mite crossed the border from Mexico. A national honey bee tracheal mite survey began, and within five months the mite had been identified in eight other states.

Several other species of external mites infest honey bees in the United States and elsewhere, but the extent of such damage has not been measured. Some mites found in honey bee colonies in other countries, particularly in the tropics, cause serious injury to developing brood.

Nosema disease. Nosema disease is an infection of the digestive organs of the adult bee by a single-celled organism, a protozoan called *Nosema apis.* Small numbers of infected bees may be found at almost any time of year in apiaries throughout the United States. The natural defenses of the individual and the colony against disease tend to keep it under control. However, when the bees are confined to the hives by poor spring weather, or subjected to stress from moving or special manipulations, such as those for queen rearing and for shaking package bees, the disease may reach damaging levels. The lives of infected bees are shortened, and affected colonies are weakened but rarely killed.

Nosema-infected colonies do not show any symptoms that are typical of the disease. For this reason, positive diagnosis can be made only by examination of bees for the presence of spores of *Nosema apis.* To do this, ground-up abdomens or alimentary tracts must be examined under a microscope at 400× magnification to detect the organism.

The disease is cyclical in its severity in the colony, with the greatest infection in late spring and the least in late summer or fall. It can be controlled, at least in part, by feeding the antibiotic fumagillin (Fumidil B). Complete control is difficult because of the chronic nature of this infection in the bee's alimentary canal. The antibiotic must be available to the bees for a considerable time to rid them of the organism. The spores of the nosema organism are spread within and outside the colony with food and water. Infected bees soil the combs and spread infection within the colony. However, nosema infection does not cause dysentery, but bees suffering from dysentery may or may not have nosema disease.

Empty combs contaminated with spores may be heated to 120°F. (49°C.) for 24 hours to kill the spores. Treatment is worthwhile; it reduces winter losses and creates stronger colonies in the spring. Treated colonies may also produce more honey. The antibiotic is most effective if fed in the fall when the normal level of the disease is lowest. Treatment in the spring is less effective but may be of value for nucleus or package colonies.

Dysentery. Although it is not a disease, dysentery is considered here because so many beekeepers think of it as a disease symptom, especially of nosema disease. Bees with dysentery are unable to hold their waste products in their bodies and they release them in the hive or close to it. The condition is recognized by the dark spots and streaks on combs, on the exterior of the hive, and on the snow near the hive in late winter (Fig. 72). Dysentery is caused by an excessive amount of water in a bee's body. The consumption during the winter of coarsely granulated honey or honey with a high water content is one cause of the disease. Damp hive conditions may also contribute to the problem. Good food and proper wintering conditions are important to prevent the problem but there is no specific control for it once the bees are affected. The colony's recovery may be helped if it is given combs of low-moisture honey or fed heavy sugar syrup. Combs from colonies with dysentery can be used safely in other colonies.

Dysentery of bees is indicated by the spotting of the hive and the snow around it in late winter. (Fig. 72)

Paralysis. Paralysis is the name given to several similar ailments of bees caused by viruses. Affected bees often shake and twitch and are unable to fly. In some cases the infected bees die within a day or two; in others, the life of the bee may only be shortened to about two-thirds its usual length. Normal bees may pull and bite the infected bees, causing their bodies to be partially hairless and shiny. The abdomens of such bees may also be enlarged. At present there are no special controls except to requeen the colony with a queen from a totally unrelated strain of bees. There appear to be distinct differences in susceptibility of different lines, races, and strains of honey bees to the viruses.

Other diseases of adult bees. Adult bees also suffer from other diseases such as septicemia and amoeba disease. Both are extremely rare and of little importance in the United States.

Pests of Honey Bees

Wax moths. The greater wax moth, *Galleria mellonella,* is a serious pest of honey comb in most areas of the United States. The adult moths are gray-brown and about ¾ inch long. In the daytime they are usually seen resting with their wings folded like a tent over their bodies (Fig. 73). When disturbed, the moths usually run rapidly before taking flight. They lay their eggs on unprotected honey combs and in the cracks between hive bodies of colonies of bees. The grayish-white larvae (Fig. 74) are kept under control by the bees in normal colonies and do no harm. They may completely ruin the combs in weak or dead colonies and in stored equipment. Unless they are controlled, they feed on the

Adult greater wax moths in a typical resting position on comb foundation. (Fig. 73)

cocoons, cast skins, and pollen in the combs, and reduce them to a mass of webs and waste products (Fig. 75). Keeping strong colonies and protecting stored equipment (see page 108) are the best ways to avoid damage from wax moth.

Several other less common moth larvae are sometimes found in combs. They usually feed only on the pollen in individual cells and are rarely pests. Fumigation and treatment for greater wax moth controls all such moths.

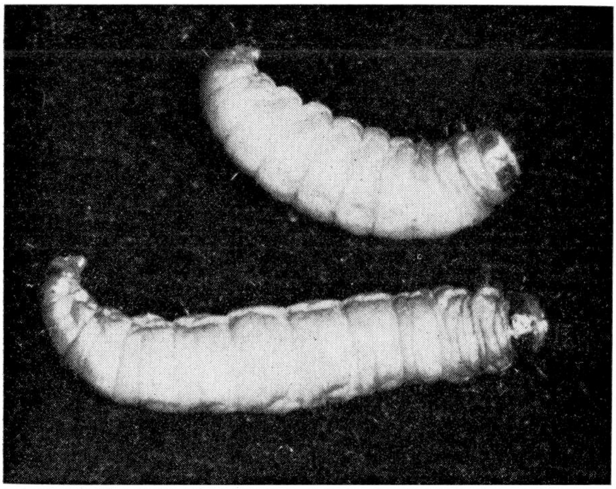

Larvae of the greater wax moth, nearly full grown. (Fig. 74)

A stored comb ruined by feeding of wax moth larvae. Cocoons are visible among the webbing and on the frame top at the bottom of the illustration. (Fig. 75)

Mice. Mice are a pest of stored combs and unoccupied combs in bee hives, usually in the fall and winter. They chew the combs, eat pollen, and build nests among the combs. In the late fall, hive entrances should be reduced to 3/8 inch in depth either by entrance cleats or by reversing the bottom board to the shallow side. Excluders or tight covers on stacks of stored combs will help to keep them mouse-free. Since mice may chew into the supers, storage areas should be protected with bait boxes containing an effective mouse poison. In apiaries where mice are a serious problem, poison bait may be placed beneath the hives or in bait boxes within an empty hive. Use all poisons with care, keep them out of reach of children, and follow the directions on the labels.

Skunks. Skunks feed on bees at night by scratching at the front of the hive and eating the bees as they come out to investigate the disturbance. People rarely trap skunks for their pelts, and the animals are increasing in numbers in many areas. It is not unusual to find several in one apiary. The skunks weaken the colonies by eating large numbers of bees and are most damaging in the fall and winter after brood rearing has ceased. They also make the colonies mean and difficult to handle. If a colony suddenly stings more often and more bees fly around your veil, look for scratching in the soil at the front corners of the hives. Where skunks are numerous, they may dig enough to leave a trench in front of the hive. Their presence can also be detected by fecal pellets that are composed largely of honey bee remains. Control skunks by trapping or poisoning them according to recommendations of your county agent or extension adviser.

Other pests of bees. Ants, toads, bears, birds, dragonflies, and other animals prey on bees. Ants can be controlled by treating their nests with an approved insecticide. Such materials are generally highly toxic to bees and should not be used close to the hives. Single colonies can be placed on stands or benches protected by oil or sticky barriers. The other pests are generally not a problem in the Midwest. However, purple martins eat bees as well as other insects and may weaken colonies in areas where there are large numbers of nesting sites. Woodpeckers and flickers sometimes make holes in hives.

Human beings are often a serious pest of bees kept in outapiaries. They may tip the hives over with their cars or by hand, shoot holes in them, or steal honey and leave the hive covers off. Apiaries should be visited regularly to watch for such damage. The problem may be lessened by posting your name and address in the apiary in a conspicuous place.

Pesticides and Honey Bees

Toxicity of pesticides. Many materials that are used to control insects, weeds, and plant diseases are toxic to honey bees. These pesticides are placed in three groups in relation to their effects on bees. *Highly toxic*** materials are those that kill bees on contact during application and for one or more days after treatment. Bees should be moved from the area if highly toxic materials are used on plants the bees are visiting. Among the materials in this group are the following:

(Trade name and/or common name)

aldrin
Ambush, permethrin
arsenicals
Avermectin
Azodrin, monocrotophos
Baygon, propoxur
Baytex, fenthion
Bidrin, dicrotophos
Bux, bufencarb
carbosulfan, FMC-35001
Cygon, dimethoate
Cythion, malathion
Dasanit, fensulfothion
DDVP, dichlorvos
Dibrom, naled*
Decis, decamethrin
De-Fend, dimethoate
diazinon, Spectracide
dieldrin
Dimecron, phosphamidon
Dursban, chlorpyrifos
Ekamet, etrimfos
EPN
Ethyl Guthion, azinphos-ethyl
Famophos, famphur
Ficam, bendiocarb
Folithion, fenitrothion
Furadan, carbofuran
Gardona, tetrachlorvinphos
Guthion, azinphos-methyl
heptachlor
Imidan, phosmet
Lannate, methomyl
Lorsban, chlorpyrifos
malathion
Matacil, aminocarb
Mesurol, methiocarb
methyl parathion
Monitor, methamidophos
Nemacur, fenamiphos
Nudrin, methomyl
Orthene, acephate
parathion
Pay-Off, flucythrinate
Phosdrin, mevinphos*
Pounce, permethrin
Pydrin, fenvalerate
Sevin, carbaryl
Spectracide, diazinon
Sumithion, fenitrothion
Sumithrin, d-phenothrin
Supracide, methidathion
Synthrin, resmethrin
Tamaron, methamidophos
Temik, aldicarb
tepp*
Vapona, dichlorvos

* Short residual activity. Can usually be applied safely when bees are not in flight. Do not apply over hives.

*Moderately toxic*** materials can be used with limited damage to bees if they are not applied over bees in the field or at the hives. Correct dosage, timing, and method of application are essential. This group includes the following:

(Trade name and/or common name)

Abate, temephos
Agritox, trichloronate
Bolstar, sulprophos
Carzol, formetanate hydrochloride
chlordane
Ciodrin, crotoxyphos
Counter, terbufos
Croneton, ethiofencarb
Curacron, profenofos
DDT
Di-Syston, disulfoton
Dyfonate, fonofos
endrin
Korlan, ronnel
Larvin, thiodicarb
Metasystox-R, oxydemethon-methyl
Mocap, ethoprop
Perthane, ethylan
Pyramat
Sevin 4-Oil, carbaryl
Sevimol, carbaryl
Systox, demeton
Thimet, phorate
Thiodan, endosulfan
Trithion, carbophenothion
Vydate, oxamyl
Zolone, phosalone

The greatest number of materials are included in the *relatively nontoxic group.*** These pesticides can be used around bees with few precautions and a minimum of injury to bees. The following list includes *some* of the materials in this group:

Insecticides and Acaricides (trade name and/or common name)

Acaraben, chlorobenzilate
allethrin, Pynamin
Altosid, methoprene
Baam, amitraz
Bacillus thuringiensis, Bactur, Bactospeine, Bakthane, Dipel, Thuricide
Birlane, chlorfenvinphos
Delnav, dioxathion
Dessin, dinobuton
Dimilin, diflubenzuron
Dylox, trichlorfon
ethion
Fundal, chlordimeform
Galecron, chlordimeform
Heliothis polyhedrosis virus
Kelthane, dicofol
Mavrik, fluvalinate
methoxychlor, Marlate
Mitac, amitraz
Morestan, oxythioquinox
Morocide, binapacryl
Murvesco, fenson
nicotine
Pentac, dienochlor
Plictran, cyhexatin
pyrethrum (natural)
rotenone
sabadilla
Sevin XLR, carbaryl
Tedion, tetradifon
Torak, dialifor
toxaphene

Fungicides (trade name and/or common name)

Benlate, benomyl
Bordeaux mixture
Bravo, chlorothalonil
captan
copper oxychloride sulfate
Cyprex, dodine
cupric hydroxide, Kocide
Difolatan, captafol
Dithane M-22, maneb
Dithane Z-78, zineb
Du-Ter, fentin hydroxide
Dyrene, anilazine
ferbam
glyodin
Karathane, dinocap
Morestan, oxythioquinox
Mylone, dazomet
sulfur
Vitavax, carboxin
ziram, Zerlate

Herbicides, Defoliants, and Desiccants (trade name and/or common name)

AAtrex, atrazine
Amiben, chloramben
Ammate, AMS
Balan, benefin
Banvel, dicamba
Bladex, cyanazine
2,4-D
dinoseb, dinitrobutylphenol
Hyvar, bromacil
Kerb, pronamide
Lasso, alachlor
Lorox, linuron
Pramitol, prometon
Princep, simazine
Prowl, pendimethalin
Sencor, metribuzin
Surflan, oryzalin
Sutan+, butylate
Telvar, monuron
Treflan, trifluralin

** Information extracted from Division of Agricultural Sciences, University of California, Leaflet 2883, February 1981, entitled "Protecting Honey Bees from Pesticides."

Pesticides damage colonies in several ways. Most often they kill the field bees without other effects on the colony. In some instances the bees die in large numbers after returning to the hive. Many bees are also lost in the field and the colony is weakened but not usually killed. Sometimes materials are carried by the bees to the hive where they kill brood, young bees, or the entire colony. Encapsulated pesticides, such as Penncap-M, have this potential of being carried to the hive.

Methods of application. Losses from pesticides can be minimized by cooperation among beekeepers, farmers, and spray operators. Several basic principles should be followed to prevent losses of bees and to avoid injury to people and farm animals. The first of these is to apply the proper dosages and follow the recommendations on the label. The method of application is also a factor to consider. Ground application is generally safer than air application. The material and its formulation play important roles in its toxicity to bees. In general, sprays are safer than dusts, and emulsifiable concentrates are less toxic than wettable powders. Materials applied as granules are the least hazardous. At present there are no safe, effective repellents that can be used to keep bees away from treated areas.

Proper timing of applications of pesticides allows the use of moderately toxic materials on crops visited by bees. Bees visit different crops at different times and for different periods during the day. The timing of treatment of a crop should relate to these bee visits. Squashes, pumpkins, and melons are attractive to bees early in the day but close their blossoms in the afternoon. Afternoon and evening treatments, after the flowers close, are safest for bees. Sweet corn sheds pollen early and is visited by bees most heavily in the morning. Applications of insecticides to sweet corn are least dangerous when made as late as possible in the day, especially if the insecticide is kept off the tassels.

For most crops, pesticide applications are safest for bees if they are made between 7 p.m. and 7 a.m.

The beekeeper's obligation. Beekeepers have responsibilities in preventing losses to their bees and in learning to accept some damage, especially in providing pollination services. In some areas, honey bee losses must be anticipated and the risk weighed against the possible returns from honey or pollination fees. Beekeepers should be familiar with commonly used pesticides and their toxicity to bees. They should know as much as possible about the relationships between their bees and the nectar and pollen plants in their territory.

It is essential that the owners of bees can be located easily when a nearby crop or the surrounding area is being treated with toxic materials. Therefore, a beekeeper should provide his or her name, address, and telephone number to owners of land on which the bees are located. This information should also be posted in the apiary in large, readable letters. Beekeepers' organizations should compile directories of apiary locations and their owners in each county, and make them available, together with marked maps, at the office of the county extension adviser or county agent.

POLLINATION BY HONEY BEES

Pollination is the transfer of pollen grains, the male sex cells of a flower, from the anther where they are produced to the receptive surface, or stigma, of the female organ of a flower. Since the honey bee is the most important insect that transfers pollen between flowers and between plants, the word "pollination" is often used to describe the service of providing bees to pollinate crop plants. This service is now more important than ever in the Midwest because the acreage of insect-pollinated crops is large as compared with the number of all kinds of bees (honey bees, bumble bees, and solitary bees) that are available to provide pollination. In many states the estimated number of colonies (hives) of bees has dropped drastically in recent years. For example, in Illinois the estimated number of hives dropped from 101,000 in 1964 to 46,000 in 1984. These two figures are probably much more accurate than some of the older, larger estimates that may have reflected state pride more than reality. Because of the reduction in numbers of bees, growers in any state can no longer assume that there are sufficient numbers of bees nearby to produce the best possible crop from insect-pollinated plants.

Honey bees are good pollinators for many reasons. Their hairy bodies trap pollen and carry it between flowers. The bees require large quantities of nectar and pollen to rear their young, and they visit flowers regularly in large numbers to obtain these foods. In doing so, they concentrate on one species of plant at a time and serve as good pollinators for this reason. Their body size enables them to pollinate flowers of many different shapes and sizes. The pollination potential of the bees is increased because they can be managed to develop high populations. The number of colonies can also be increased as needed and the colonies can be moved to the most desirable location for pollination purposes.

Honey bees are most active at temperatures between 60°F. (16°C.) and 105°F. (41°C.). Winds above 15 miles per hour reduce their activity and stop it completely at about 25 miles per hour. When conditions for flight are not ideal, honey bees work close to their colonies. Although they may fly as far as 5 miles in search of food, they usually go no farther than 1 to 1½ miles in good weather. In unfavorable weather, bees may visit only those plants nearest the hive. They also tend to work closer to the hive in areas where there are large numbers of attractive plants in bloom.

The following midwestern crops must be pollinated by bees to produce fruit or seed:

- Alfalfa
- Apple
- Apricot
- Blackberry
- Blueberry
- Cherry
- Clovers
  - Sweetclovers, white and yellow
  - True clovers
    - Alsike
    - Ladino
    - Red
    - White Dutch
- Cranberry
- Cucumber
- Muskmelon, cantaloupe
- Nectarine
- Peach
- Pear
- Persimmon, native
- Plum, prune
- Pumpkin
- Raspberry
- Squash
- Sunflower
- Trefoil
- Watermelon

The following crops set fruit or seed without insect visits but yields and quality may be improved by honey bees:

- Eggplant
- Grape
- Lespedeza
- Lima bean
- Okra
- Pepper
- Soybean
- Strawberry

Honey bees visit several important crops but do not improve their yields of fruit or seed. These include the following:

- Field bean
- Pea
- String or snap bean
- Sweet corn

The provision of bees for pollination of crop plants is a specialized practice, not just a sideline of honey production. Beekeepers who supply bees for pollination must learn the skills of management that are necessary for success in this phase of beekeeping. Such skills include the development and selection of strong colonies that are able to provide the large force of field bees needed to do the job of transferring pollen. This task of the beekeeper is hardest to accomplish for fruit pollination early in the year. Each beekeeper or organization of beekeepers should set minimum standards for colony strength and size to use as a basis for establishing prices and for providing the best possible service. The number of bees, and not the number of hives, is the true unit of measure, and growers need to be told and shown what standards are being used to measure the honey bee colonies for pollination. For example, colonies for apple pollination should be housed in a two-story hive with a laying queen. There should be four or more frames with brood and sufficient bees to cover them. There should also be a reserve food supply of 10 pounds of honey or more. Colonies rented to pollinate crops that bloom later in the year should be proportionately stronger, with five or six frames with brood, approximately 600 to 800 square inches. In the field, the colonies must be supered and examined at intervals to keep them in suitable condition for pollination.

The number of standard colonies that are needed per acre of crop plants varies in relation to the attractiveness of the crop, the competition from surrounding sources of nectar and pollen, and the percentage of flowers that must produce fruit or seed to provide an economic return. Most crops are adequately pollinated by one strong hive of bees per acre. However, red clover grown for seed should have two or more colonies per acre moved to the field as soon as it begins to bloom (Fig. 76). Alfalfa requires three to five colonies per acre. Hybrid cumumbers grown at plant populations of 40,000 to 70,000 or more plants per acre for machine harvest may require up to four hives per acre. The higher number of hives may be needed where other cultivated plants or weeds compete strongly for the attention of the bees.

Pollination of second-crop red clover for seed. Honey bees are effective pollinators of red clover in July and August when other clovers have ceased to bloom. Illinois produces large quantities of red clover seed, often as much as one-sixth of the total production in the United States. (Fig. 76)

Honey bee hives placed in groups in an apple orchard in southern Illinois. (Fig. 77)

Bees for pollination should be placed within or beside the crop to be pollinated. For apples, place groups of 5 to 15 hives at intervals of 200 to 300 yards (Fig. 77). They should be moved into the orchard at 10 to 25 percent bloom. For cucumbers and other cucurbits, bees should be moved to the field when the first female flowers appear, not before. Place the bees in a single group for small fields. For fields larger than 30 acres, place the bees in two or more groups at the edges of the field but leave no more than 1/10 mile between groups. Bees seem to work better upwind from their hives than downwind, so it is probably worthwhile to locate more colonies on the downwind side of the field or orchard than on the side from which the wind blows.

Bees need a nearby source of water such as a farm pond or a stock tank with cork or wooden floats on which they can land. Water is important in the early spring for brood rearing and later for cooling the hives. In fruit pollination the bees benefit from full sun and shelter from the wind. Later in the year, some afternoon shade is helpful.

Contracts for honey bee pollination services should be a regular part of the business when more than a few hives are involved. Contracts prevent problems that may arise from misunderstanding, and they serve to emphasize the obligations and rights of both grower and beekeeper. Contracts should include provisions relating to pesticide usage, colony standards and the rights of the grower to examine the colonies, rights of access by the beekeeper, pollination fees and time of payment, and a statement about the timing of movements of bees to and from the crop.

Colony rental fees vary in relation to the expenses involved and the length of time the colonies are needed. The potential or actual honey production of the rented colonies is also a factor in establishing prices for summer-blooming crops, with higher prices for less productive plant species. Additional moves and the movement of colonies by growers may increase or lower the price. The *Honey Market News* (see page 94) publishes typical prices being charged for pollination services.

SELECTED SOURCES OF INFORMATION ON BEEKEEPING AND EQUIPMENT

Books, Handbooks, and Manuals

Bailey, L. 1963. Infectious diseases of the honey-bee. Land Books, Ltd., London. 176 p. Out of print.

Butler, C. G. 1974. The world of the honeybee. 3rd ed. Collins, London. 226 p.

Crane. E., ed. 1975. Honey: a comprehensive survey. Crane, Russak & Co., New York. 608 p.

Dadant & Sons, ed. 1975. The hive and the honey bee. 4th ed. Dadant & Sons, Inc., Hamilton, Illinois. 740 p.

Dade, H. A. 1962. Anatomy and dissection of the honeybee. Bee Research Association, London. 158 p. + 20 foldout plates.

Eckert, J. E., and F. R. Shaw. 1960. Beekeeping. The Macmillan Co., New York. 536 p.

Free, J. B. 1970. Insect pollination of crops. Academic Press, New York. 544 p.

Free, J. B. 1977. The social organization of honeybees. Edward Arnold, London. 68 p.

Frisch, K. von. 1967. The dance language and orientation of bees. Belknap Press, Cambridge, Massachusetts. 566 p.

Frisch, K. von. 1971. Bees. Their vision, chemical senses, and language. 2nd ed. Cornell University Press, Ithaca, New York. 157 p.

Howes, F. N. 1979. Plants and beekeeping. Faber and Faber, London. 256 p.

Jaycox, E. R. 1982. Beekeeping tips and topics. The Bee Specialist, Dept. D 5775, Jornada Road North, Las Cruces, New Mexico 88001.

Kelley, W. T. 1980. How to keep bees and sell honey. Walter T. Kelley Co., Clarkson, Kentucky. 144 p.

Killion, E. E. 1981. Honey in the comb. Dadant & Sons, Inc., Hamilton, Illinois. 148 p.

Laidlaw, H. H., Jr. 1979. Contemporary queen rearing. Dadant & Sons, Inc., Hamilton, Illinois. 199 p.

Lindauer, M. 1971. Communication among social bees. 3rd printing with appendices. Harvard University Press, Cambridge, Massachusetts. 161 p.

McGregor, S. E. 1976. Insect pollination of cultivated crop plants. Agriculture Handbook No. 496. U.S. Government Printing Office, Washington, D.C. 411 p.

Morse, R. A., ed. 1978. Honey bee pests, predators, and diseases. Cornell University Press, Ithaca, New York. 430 p.

Pellett, F. C. 1938. History of American beekeeping. Collegiate Press, Inc., Ames, Iowa. 213 p. Out of print.

Pellett, F. C. 1976. American honey plants. Dadant & Sons, Inc., Hamilton, Illinois. 467 p. Reprint of 1947 edition.

Root, A. I., E. R. Root, H. H. Root, and J. A. Root. 1980. The ABC and XYZ of bee culture. 38th ed. A. I. Root Company, Medina, Ohio. 732 p.

Root, H. H. 1951. Beeswax. Chemical Publishing Company, Inc., Brooklyn, New York. 154 p. Out of print.

Snodgrass, R. E. 1956. Anatomy of the honey bee. Comstock Publishing Associates, Ithaca, New York. 334 p.

U.S. Department of Agriculture. 1980. Beekeeping in the United States. U.S. Department of Agriculture Handbook 335. U.S. Government Printing Office, Washington, D.C.

White, J. W., Jr., M. L. Riethof, M. H. Subers, and I. Kushnir. 1962. Composition of American honeys. U.S. Department of Agriculture Technical Bulletin 1261. U.S. Government Printing Office, Washington, D.C. 124 p.

Periodicals

American Bee Journal. Hamilton, Illinois 62341. Monthly.

Bee World. Hill House, Chalfont St. Peter, Gerrards Cross, Bucks., England SL9 ONR. Quarterly.

Gleanings in Bee Culture. Medina, Ohio 44256. Monthly.

The Speedy Bee. Route 1, Box G-27, Jesup, Georgia 31545. Monthly newspaper.

Beekeeping Organizations

American Beekeeping Federation, Inc., 13637 N.W. 39th Avenue, Gainesville, Florida 32601.

American Honey Producers Association, Inc., Box 368, Minco, Oklahoma 73059.

Write to your extension beekeeping specialist or state apiary inspector for current addresses for state and local beekeeping associations. In Illinois, write to Extension Beekeeping Specialist, 172 Natural Resources Building, University of Illinois at Urbana-Champaign, 607 E. Peabody Drive, Champaign, Illinois 61820.

Beekeeping Supplies and Equipment

Dadant & Sons, Inc. Hamilton, Illinois 62341.

Hubbard Apiaries. Onsted, Michigan 49265.

Walter T. Kelley Co. Clarkson, Kentucky 42726.

A. I. Root Co. Medina, Ohio 44256 and Council Bluffs, Iowa 51501.

For sources of package bees and queens consult current issues of beekeeping magazines.

Apiary Inspection, Registration, and Beekeeping Information

In most states, apiary inspection and registration are carried out by employees of the state Department of Agriculture. They can provide information about laws relating to bee diseases, registration, and movement of colonies. They may also be able to provide inspection and diagnosis of bee disease samples on request. For such services in Illinois, write the Chief Apiary Inspector, 522 South Jefferson, Paris, Illinois 61944.

Beekeeping and pollination information is available through the Cooperative Extension Service at the college of agriculture of the land grant university in each state. Extension apiculturists or entomologists are available in every state. In Illinois, help is available from the Extension Beekeeping Specialist, 172 Natural Resources Building, University of Illinois at Urbana-Champaign, 607 E. Peabody Drive, Champaign, Illinois 61820.

The U.S. Department of Agriculture publishes information about bees and beekeeping and provides laboratory diagnosis for adult and brood diseases of bees. Requests for information and samples for examination can be sent to the Bioenvironmental Bee Laboratory, USDA-SEA, Building 476, BARC-East, Beltsville, Maryland 20705.

GLOSSARY

Abdomen — the last major body region of the bee, one of three regions.

Acarine disease — a disease of adult bees caused by a mite, *Acarapis woodi,* infesting the tracheae.

Adrenalin — a drug used for treatment of severe reactions to bee stings; also called epinephrine.

Alimentary canal or tract — the passage in the bee's body that food passes through from mouth to anus.

American foulbrood (AFB) — an infectious disease of immature honey bees caused by a bacterium, *Bacillus larvae.*

Apiary — a place where bees are kept.

Apiculture — beekeeping.

Balling — the clustering of bees tightly around a queen bee, usually in an attempt to kill her.

Bee blower — a portable machine that produces large volumes of rapidly moving air to blow bees from combs.

Bee brush — a soft-bristled brush used for removing bees from combs.

Bee escape — a tube through which bees can move in only one direction.

Bee space — a ¼- to ⅜-inch space through which a bee can move freely; the space between the frames and exterior parts of a hive. Bees will not build comb in it or seal it with propolis, thereby allowing the frames to be removed easily.

Bee veil — a wire screen or cloth enclosure worn over the head and neck to protect them from bee stings.

Beeswax — a substance secreted from glands on the bee's abdomen that is used to construct comb.

Benzaldehyde — a liquid used to drive bees from honey combs; a component of oil of bitter almond. It has a smell that is pleasant to humans.

Boardman feeder — see entrance feeder.

Bottom board — the floor of a hive.

Brood — the immature stages of the bee (egg, larva, and pupa) considered together.

Brood chamber — the part of the hive in which young bees are reared. It usually includes one or two hive bodies with combs.

Brood nest — the area within the combs in which young bees are reared. It may include only part of one comb or many combs.

Burr comb — small pieces of comb built between combs and parts of the hive.

Butyric anhydride — a liquid used to drive bees from honey combs. It has an odor unpleasant for humans similar to that found in rancid butter and perspiration.

Carniolan bee — a dark honey bee race originating in southeastern Europe.

Castes — the different forms of adult female bees in a colony; workers and queens.

Caucasian bee — a dark honey bee race originating in the Caucasus.

Cell — a single compartment in a honey comb.

Certan — a biological insecticide developed specifically for the control of wax moth.

Chunk honey — a piece or pieces of comb honey packed in a jar with liquid extracted honey.

Cleansing flight — bee flight, after a period of confinement, to dispose of feces or body wastes.

Colony — an entire honey bee family or social unit living together in a hive or other shelter.

Comb — a beeswax structure composed of two layers of horizontal cells sharing their bases, usually within a wooden frame in a hive. The words "comb" and "frame" are often used interchangeably; for example, a frame of brood, a comb of brood.

Comb foundation — a sheet of beeswax embossed on each side with the cell pattern.

Comb honey — honey in the sealed comb in which it was produced; also called section comb honey when produced in thin wooden frames called sections, and bulk comb honey when produced in shallow frames.

Creamed honey — finely granulated honey produced by adding fine honey crystals to liquid honey.

Cucurbit — a plant in the family Cucurbitaceae, which includes squash, pumpkin, watermelon, muskmelon, and cucumber.

Cut comb honey — a portion of comb honey cut from a larger comb.

Division-board feeder — a waterproof, plastic or wooden syrup container the size of a frame, used to feed bees within the hive.

Division screen — a wooden frame with two layers of wire screen that serves to separate two colonies within the same hive, one above the other.

Draw — to shape and build, as to draw comb.

Drawn comb — a comb constructed on a sheet of foundation.

Drifting — the return of field bees to colonies other than their own.

Drone layer, drone-laying queen — a queen that is unable to lay fertilized eggs because of failure to mate or lack of sufficient spermatozoa; a queen whose eggs produce drones in worker cells.

Dysentery — a malady of adult bees marked by an accumulation of excess feces or waste products, and by their release in and near the hive.

Entrance feeder — a wooden runway that fits into the hive entrance so that bees may obtain syrup from a jar inverted into it.

Enzyme — an organic substance produced in plant or animal cells that causes changes in other substances by catalytic action.

Epinephrine — see adrenalin.

European foulbrood (EFB) — an infectious disease of immature honey bees caused by a bacterium, *Streptococcus pluton.*

Excluder — a thin grid of wire, wood and wire, sheet plastic, or sheet zinc, with spaces wide enough for workers to pass through but not queens or drones. It is used between hive bodies to confine queens to one part of a hive.

Extracted honey — liquid honey removed from the comb by means of an extractor or other methods of separation.

Extractor (honey extractor) — a hand- or power-driven device that removes honey from the comb by centrifugal force.

Field bee (forager) — worker bee that collects nectar, pollen, water, and propolis at locations outside the hive.

Foulbrood — a general name for infectious diseases of immature bees that cause them to die and their remains to smell bad. The term most often refers to American foulbrood.

Foundation — see comb foundation.

Frame — a wooden rectangle that surrounds the comb and hangs within the hive. It may be referred to as Hoffman, Langstroth, or self-spacing because of differences in size and widened end bars that provide a bee space between the combs. The words "frame" and "comb" are often used interchangeably; for example, a comb of brood, a frame of brood.

Fume board — a general name for any shallow wooden cover used to hold repellents for driving bees from honey combs.

Fumigant — a material that acts as a disinfectant or pesticide in a gaseous form when exposed to air.

Genetic or hereditary makeup — the characteristics of an individual inherited from its parents.

Granulated honey — honey in which crystals of a sugar (dextrose) have formed.

Granulation — the formation of sugar (dextrose) crystals in honey.

Head — the first major body region of an insect, bearing the eyes. antennae, and mouthparts.

Hive — a wooden box or other container in which a honey bee colony lives.

Hive body — a single wooden rim or shell that holds a set of frames. When used for the brood nest, it is called a brood chamber; when used above the brood nest for honey storage, it is called a super. It may be of various widths and heights and adapted for comb honey sections.

Hive cover — the roof or lid of a hive.

Hive loader — a mechanically operated boom and cradle for manipulating hives and placing them on a truck.

Hive tool — a metal bar used to loosen frames and to separate the parts of a hive.

Honey — a sweet, viscid fluid produced by honey bees from nectar collected from flowers.

Honeydew — a sweet liquid, primarily plant sap, excreted by plant-feeding insects and often collected by honey bees.

Honey flow — see nectar flow.

House bee — a young worker bee, 1 day to 2 weeks old, that works only in the hive.

Hybrid bees — the offspring resulting from crosses of two or more selected inbred lines (strains) of bees; the offspring of crosses between races of bees.

Inbreeding — a breeding system that features mating of related individuals.

Inner cover — a thin wooden hive lid used beneath a telescoping cover.

Italian bee — a yellow honey bee race originating in Italy.

Langstroth hive — a hive with movable frames made possible by the bee space around them. It was invented by L. L. Langstroth.

Larva, larvae — the grublike or wormlike immature form of an insect; the second stage in metamorphosis.

Laying worker — a worker bee that produces eggs that normally develop into drones.

Legume — the common name for plants of the pea family, Leguminosae, including clover, sweetclover, vetch, alfalfa, and many other nectar and pollen plants.

Metamorphosis — the series of changes through which an insect passes from the egg to larva, pupa, and adult.

Nectar — a sweet liquid secreted by plant glands (nectaries) usually located in flowers, but also found on other parts of plants.

Nectar flow — the period when abundant nectar is available for bees to produce honey for storage in the combs of the hive.

Nosema disease — an infectious disease of adult bees caused by a protozoan, *Nosema apis.*

Nuc — abbreviation for nucleus.

Nuc box — a small hive used for housing a small colony or nucleus.

Nucleus, nuclei — a small colony of bees with a queen and enough workers to cover two to five frames or combs.

Nurse bee — a young bee, usually 2 to 10 days old, that feeds and cares for immature bees.

Outapiary — an apiary located some distance from the beekeeper's home.

Ovary — the egg-producing part of the female reproductive system.

Package bees — 2 to 4 pounds of worker bees, usually with a queen, in a screen-sided wooden cage with a can of sugar syrup for food.

Pallet — a cleated wooden stand on which supers are stacked for bulk handling; also used to hold two to seven hives for moving, especially for pollination service.

Paradichlorobenzene (PDB) — a white crystalline substance used to fumigate combs and to repel wax moths.

Paralysis — a disease of adult bees caused by a virus.

Pentachlorophenol (penta) — a wood preservative that has been used for hive parts but is generally no longer recommended.

Pesticide — a general name for materials used to kill undesirable insects, plants, rodents, and other pests.

Pfund color grader — an instrument used to classify the color of samples of liquid honey.

pH — a symbol for a measure of relative acidity or alkalinity of solutions; values below 7 are acid, values above 7 are alkaline.

Pistil — the female part of a flower that includes the ovary, style, and stigma.

Play flight — short flight in front of the hive taken by young bees when they first leave the hive; an orientation flight.

Pollen — male sex cells, usually very small and powdery, produced in the anthers of a flower.

Pollen basket — an area on a bee's hind leg where pollen is packed and carried with help from a central spine and surrounding hairs.

Pollen insert — a device placed in the hive entrance to apply live pollen to outgoing bees for cross-pollination, as in apples.

Pollen substitute — a mixture of materials such as soy flour, casein, brewers' yeast, and dried milk fed to bees to stimulate brood rearing.

Pollen supplement — a mixture of pollen substitute and pollen fed to bees to stimulate brood rearing.

Pollen trap — a device that removes pollen pellets from bees' legs as they enter the hive.

Pollination — the transfer of pollen from the anther to the stigma, the receptive surface of the female organ of a flower; in beekeeping terms, pollination often refers to the service of providing bees for pollination of crop plants.

Pollinator — an agent, such as an insect, that transfers pollen.

Pollinizer — a plant that furnishes pollen to another plant.

Propolis — plant resins collected from plants by bees to use in sealing cracks and crevices in hives; bee glue.

Pupa, pupae — the inactive third stage in the complete metamorphosis of an insect. The adult body form is evident at this stage.

Queen-cage candy — a firm mixture of powdered sugar and liquid invert sugar used in queen cages as food for the queen and her attendant bees.

Queen excluder — see excluder.

Queenless colony — a honey bee colony without a queen.

Queenright colony — a honey bee colony with a queen.

Rabbet — a piece of wood or metal on which the frame ends hang in the hive; a cutout area used as a frame rest.

Refractometer — an instrument for measuring the percent of soluble solids in a solution, designed to read directly in percent moisture; used for measuring the percent moisture in honey and nectar.

Reproductive system — the organs of the body, either male or female, concerned with producing offspring.

Requeening — removal of a queen from a colony and introduction of a new one.

Robber bee — a field bee from one colony that takes, or tries to take, honey from another colony.

Robbing — the stealing of honey from a colony by bees from another colony.

Royal jelly — a mixture of glandular secretions of worker bees fed to developing queens.

Sacbrood — a virus disease of immature honey bees.

Scale colony — a hive that is maintained on a scale and whose weight changes are measured and recorded daily or at other frequent intervals.

Scout bee — a field bee that locates new sources of food, water, or propolis, or a new home for a swarm.

Sealed brood — immature bees in their late larval and pupal stages within capped cells of the comb.

Section comb honey — honey in sealed comb produced in thin plastic or wooden frames called sections.

Sex alleles — hereditary characteristics of bees that, in part, determine the sex of the individual bee.

Slumgum — the refuse from melted combs after all or part of the wax is removed.

Smoker — a steel container with an attached bellows in which burning materials furnish smoke to repel and subdue honey bees.

Social bees — bees that live in groups or colonies, such as bumble bees, stingless bees, and honey bees.

Solar wax melter (solar extractor) — a glass-covered box used for melting combs and cappings by heat from the sun.

Solitary bees — bees that live alone and whose offspring individually survive the winter, usually in an immature stage in a cell in the ground or a variety of other sites.

Spiracles — the openings to an insect's internal breathing tubes, the tracheae.

Stigma — the receptive surface of the female organ of a flower that receives the pollen.

Super — a hive body used for honey storage above the brood chambers of a hive.

Supering — placing supers of comb or foundation on a hive, either to give more room for brood rearing or for honey storage.

Supersedure — replacement by the bees of an established queen with a new one without swarming.

Swarm — a group of worker bees and a queen (usually the old one) that leave the hive to establish a new colony; a word formerly used to describe a hive or colony of bees.

Telescoping cover — a hive cover, used with an inner cover, that extends downward several inches on all four sides of a hive.

Thorax — the middle body region of an insect to which the wings and legs are attached.

Trachea, tracheae — the breathing tube of an insect.

Transferring — moving bees and comb from a natural nest in a cavity or container to a movable frame hive.

Uncapping — cutting a thin layer from a comb surface to remove the wax covering from sealed cells of honey.

Uncapping knife — a knife, usually heated, for cutting cappings from honey comb.

Uniting — combining one honey bee colony with another.

Unsealed brood — eggs and larvae in open cells.

Virgin queen — an unmated queen.

Wax moth — an insect whose larvae feed on and destroy honey bee combs.

Wired foundation — comb foundation manufactured with vertical wires embedded in it for added strength.

Wiring — installing tinned wire in frames as support for combs.

INDEX

Issued in furtherance of Cooperative Extension Work, Acts of May 8 and June 30, 1914, in cooperation with the U.S. Department of Agriculture. WILLIAM R. OSCHWALD, Director, Cooperative Extension Service, University of Illinois at Urbana-Champaign. The Illinois Cooperative Extension Service provides equal opportunities in programs and employment.
10M—9-76—34696—MN
7M—4-81—50453—CC
5M—4-85—60885—AP